Entering the Life of the

Exquisite Past

A Memoir

What price are you willing to pay to live an additional year?

by

Joy M. Pierre

Editor: Joy M. Pierre and Gutemberg J. Pierre

Cover Design: Joy M. Pierre and Gutemberg J. Pierre

Published by Adequate Media Production

ISBN: 979-8-9892642-0-9

Library of Congress Control Number: 2023915034
Printed in the United States of America

Table of Contents

Entering the Life of the Exquisite Past

*F*or those of us who faced tragedies never forgot how they came through them. Some of us questioned the Lord, asking him if he listened to our prayers. Others felt that life had no value and they were content with negative upbringing.

You and I were never a problem. Before we were conceived, our lives were predestined. But, at times we make decisions that delay the original plan of our lives. We allow negative influences to dictate our behaviors.

We also weren't born with instructions, on how to embrace challenging experiences. But rightfully, it's our approach, which allows us to conquer anything we face. We don't have to be alone in our decisions. We only have to reach out, help is waiting for us. We deserve to exist; life is a gift. If only we were confident in ourselves, life would get better.

So, while we're thinking if broken can be fixed, and who's going to fix it for us, always remember that life has something better for you.

Chapter 1

We all have our own perception of how we value life. But can we put a price on the aftermath of it? All of us have paid a price whether it's big or small, but how much are you willing to pay to live an additional year? So, while you're thinking, do you think guns kill people or do you believe it is people that kill people?

Those who knew me or gotten to know me knew me as quiet, well mannered, observant, bold, courageous and strong. My adjustments toward different atmospheres shaped me. As for most of you who don't know me, I'm from Flint, Michigan.

Not proud to say, but I've too heard of ridiculous, shame rumors, and was known for one of the top-rated murder cities in the states. Some of it was true, and some stories were made up. I saw living there, one way and the only way of life. That was the only life I've experienced. Many of us were talented with only a few recognized for their greatness. Flint was one of the greatest places I've known. On top of things, it was my birthplace. I didn't get a chance to view the world. My outlook on life from the experiences and battles wasn't the average bear. It was difficult. I realized by being human, life would happen at the end of my comfort zone.

When we reach out to one another our first reaction on a person is ever the remark. Our intentions are to show our personality. We like to think by living, everything we could want, would come true. Likewise, none of that was true when we acted strangely.

I lived in an area that only enjoyed the sudden get rich plan. There were more whom didn't work hard, but got the job done. We all knew eating from the silver spoon made lives hard and even troubled us too. None of us lived in perfection. We all saw something, done things and experienced something at a time in our lives. Blindfolds and extra sleeping never relieved a situation, it made them worst when facing them all over again. The silence of voices, tears of pain, and most of all broken hearts, roamed the air.

I moved into my first place in a hurry because I needed a place to rest my head. While working three jobs I lost contact with all my friends because of never-ending bills. I shopped at all the local Goodwill's, hopeful to find the color tags of the week to gain an extra 50% off. Some weeks were better than others. I didn't care about who saw me, I was surviving. Shopping alone allowed me to take my time sorting through the new and rugged clothing. I took my survival tactics personal. It wasn't something I was proud of. Others asked where I purchased my nice clothes; I smiled keeping my secret. I couldn't tell them the Goodwill for crying out loud, it

Joy M. Pierre

embarrassed me. Shopping there was a norm because my pockets were never deep enough for the shopping malls. I thought by working all the jobs my money would stretch, but it didn't. One of my jobs was seasonal and the other two were regular minimum-waged that didn't provide enough to cover the rent and the utility bills. As for food, I did the best I could. Depression kicked in and my back was against the wall. I looked for many outlets but there were none.

One day after slipping and sliding on the icy roads, I arrived home from a tired day at work. I pulled up with a dropped jaw. I was silent with tears rolling down my face. I saw my things, and they weren't in the house. They were in the snow on the curb. That was a feeling no one wanted to experience. It was like having the life sucked out of you by a vacuum. It was a feeling of pure violation you couldn't escape from. There was nowhere to turn. I contacted the closest person I knew; my dad. I didn't have a close connection with him or his wife, but it was worth a try. I reached out to them and asked if I could stay until I had gotten back on my feet. The answer was no. She asked if I had any felonies. I was confused. I couldn't understand of all things; why that? I wondered if something was said about me doing wrong. Everything was happening too fast.

At the time my options were slim to none. Depression had set into my soul. Not only was I pregnant; I had nowhere to go. My car broke down so living in the car was out of the picture. As bad as I didn't want the life I owned, it was mine. I was homeless. I never thought my life would have allowed me to be such. Out of total embarrassment, I didn't want to see, talk, or hear anything anyone had to say.

That was not the life I signed up for. The worse feeling of all, I had no home or a bed to go to. I gave up and stopped talking while weight fell tremendously. I tried pulling myself together, but I kept falling at the waistline. My only option was to call two shelters in Flint. I thought of all the questions to ask and as soon as the phone rang, my mind only allowed me to ask the major two questions. "How could I get a bed" and "What would get me kicked out."

I called another one with disappointment. The main thing I needed they didn't have. They had no empty beds. So, the only choice I had was to check myself into the Carriage Town Mission.

That shelter was for women and children only. That was my only hope. I direly needed a place to stay, plus I was expecting. Mainly, they provided resources on rental properties. The first day I stood in line with others, waiting to enter. I stood there fiddling with my hands and tapping my foot. I looked at the others standing ahead of me. Women and children wore worn clothes and their shoes were filthy. As for their hair, I wanted to walk away. I knew that place wasn't the right decision. I felt it wasn't right for me to be there. I knew I was doing badly, but I didn't think it was that bad. I felt my heart beating faster, and I tapped my foot faster against the pavement. I hoped and prayed all of it was a dream. I wanted it to be a nightmare, hopeful for someone to wake me.

Indeed it was real. The doors opened and the line slowly entered the threshold. I looked behind me one more time. It was my choice and only one person could have changed my mind. I wanted someone to stop me. I kept looking back hoping and praying he was there. I saw no one. I took one last look, rubbing my stomach, enter-

Joy M. Pierre

ing the door.

I made it in, turning to look back one last time at the entrance. The staff locked the door behind us with a key. That was a punishment, and I felt imprisonment from that sound. That was close to the real meaning of bondage. It was the locking of the door that killed me. I felt that was how the prisoners were treated.

I walked moping to my room. When I arrived my roommate looked up staring. I was a stranger, and she was one too. I sat me and my small duffle bags on the bed with my back turned to her and cried. The uncomfortable bed made me panic more.

I couldn't imagine how that place could have been helpful. I knew the environment was going to be strict. We ate, bathe, was put out of our room, and left the building all at routine times. That was the way the shelter coached addicts and helped with detoxification, and I became a part of it.

I was the only pregnant one, but I still wasn't exempt. That made me no better than them. I was homeless like them dealing with similar situations. That was one thing we all could relate to. Alone in my room, I laid face down screaming and crying in the pillow. My fist punched the bed every time I raised my face from the pillow to breathe. I wanted no one to hear me. I wanted to get my frustration out with no one stopping me. Tears were my only way of cleansing my soul.

One night my painful stomach growled, and I was in a bad situation. No food was allowed from the outside. I couldn't take it anymore. I took a risk breaking the rules sneaking food in to carve my hunger. I knew it was a possibility of getting caught, but the risk was greater.

On certain days, I had no choice but to eat there. It wasn't the greatest, and it was awful at times, but I managed. I didn't have much leisure time to myself but they offered Bible study, which I didn't care for. I felt God had forgotten about me, and I knew he had sent me there to be alone, pregnant, angry, miserable, and bitter.

I found a small, cute house on the wrong side of town three months later. It was on Flint's Nutty Northside. The city had major crime issues, but at the time it was Northside of Flint. That's where my son was born. I knew having him would change some things in my life. From that day forward, I knew I had to stand up and defend for him.

That momen of my life was like any other young adult, with the lack of knowledge. I hung out with others I felt were like me because I didn't want to be alone. I used to visit and sit with others for no reason at all. I knew it was a waste of time, but I did it anyway. I involved myself in bad situations that I hated, just to feel a part of something or someone.

I saw myself hating others because I cherish things they didn't. They joked about childish situation and took life for granted. Life stopped being funny for me. I experienced some heartfelt situations and knew how bad it hurt.

I forced myself to be a loner even more. I felt others thought I needed what they had. I didn't. I smoked cigarettes because I needed to relieve stress and I knew it was wrong, but I also wanted something for myself. At the time smoking was like having a best friend down

Joy M. Pierre

for whatever.

I thought things were looking up for me. From balancing a child, relationship, working, a new place, and smoking, I still felt left out. It was still something missing. I wasn't complete. I needed more. My same daily routines drained me. My mind drifted back to a bad situation, like the days I spent at the shelter. I hated the fact that I went through it alone. I kept my feelings and emotions bottled up so others wouldn't judge me. My fake smiles carried me a long way until the stress affected my body. I knew what it felt like to be an angry person. Stress continued to take over my body. I had an episode where my eyes was bloodshot red, for unknown reasons.

I roam the city like a creature, with no clue of my surroundings. My life was miserable, and I couldn't stand the way others looked at me. After many doctor visits, my diagnosis was a severe stress disorder. The more stress that fell upon me, the more shame I felt. Years later after holding on to so much stress, I had another episode. I was at work, working with the elderly, and it was a hard day at work. I went to grab a seat to rest, my right knee popped. It was the sound of an old achy bone that snapped. I thought it was a warning sign of a hard day, so I sought no help for it.

Days later, I came home from work to a disaster. Someone broke into my house. They knew my work patterns, and I'm sure they did. I lived by others without jobs. While they robbed me, they sat and drank juice from the refrigerator and ate chips from the kitchen cabinet. I never left things out. I cleaned behind myself all the time, and that wasn't something I would do. I knew it had to be planned, because they had time to decipher through whatever it was they were looking for. Not to mention, I couldn't live another day in that house. They had strewn my undergarments all over. The only thing I could think of was that the intruders were sniffing them. That was a terrifying moment for me. I moved my things to my sister's house and bunked in with her for a while. I slept on her floor just to enjoy a peace of mind. I didn't care about having a bed, I didn't want to be alone. I was worried about someone entering my premises and take my life or forcing me to take theirs.

Exactly one month after my knee popped, I couldn't get off the floor from where I had been sleeping. My painful knee was throbbing. It was five times its normal size. I was shocked. I never saw anything like it. Calling out of work wasn't any help. I believed I had a valid reason for staying home. But as for them, it wasn't good enough, so I dragged my leg to the car and lifted it with two hands. That was the only way of getting it inside the car. I drove to work to defend my statement, before going to see my doctor. I wasn't kidding, and it wasn't a joke. But I couldn't risk losing my job. Employees called out all the time for nonsense.

Making it to the doctor's office, they sucked the life out of me by draining the fluid from my knee with an oversized syringe. From excruciating pain, I still had to drive back home. Making it close to where I was bunking, my phone rang. It was the admission department from the hospital. A lady told me there was no time to waste and that I was pre-admitted into Hurley Medical Center for an emergency surgery. The fluid they drained, was an infection that ran through my bloodstream. I took the phone off my ear looking down to see the number. She kept talking. I got back on the phone and told her she made a mistake. I thought she called the wrong person but she didn't. She assured me it was me she was looking for. Then she told me it was serious and the fluid was deadly. I was in complete shock.

My voice crackled asking information to where I was going. She kept talking. But none of it made sense because I was focused on the word surgery and deadly. I rushed to get there looking at others in line. When it was my turn, I walked up to the desk and only said my name. She rushed to the door and told me to walk that way. My shaky legs buckled. Scared was an understatement. With no time to waste, I jumped and laid on a hard stretcher bed. The staff moved fast, and I didn't understand what was going on. A nurse pushed me through double doors. I panicked. I swarmed the bed, wanting to hop off and run, but she was still pushing. I turned my head to look back to see if anyone had come with me. I was alone.

I turned back forward, stared up hoping to see Gods face to fuss at him. Unforced salty tears ran down the sides of my face, falling into my ears. That moment was surreal. My eyes closed, and I prayed. "Lord, please keep your hand over me; I don't want to die and I want to go home, please let everything go right. I want to wake up, please don't keep me asleep." Before I opened my eyes, I could hear mumbling voices surrounding me. Tools were clanking and papers raddling. Everything was happening.

I opened my eyes; I was in the operating room. The surgeon introduced himself and explained the procedure. It became even more real. So I panicked, shouting, and telling them to wait a minute. I wasn't ready yet. They weren't listening, so I kept repeating it. The surgeon reassured me and calmed me down. He told me to close my eyes, and, as soon as they're closed, he would administer the anesthesia. I knew nothing about him and I didn't trust him. A nurse calmly grabbed my hand with a smile.

She saw fright in my eyes. My anxiety level was too high for me to calm down, but the more she smiled telling me everything would be okay, calmed me. That wasn't a fact of being stubborn, I had trust issues and I thought I was protecting myself. I took a deep breath and slowly closed my eyes. I opened them back up immediately looking at the doctor with the evil eye. I wanted to ask him who he was talking to earlier. But there was no one in the room that I knew would help me. They could have done anything to me and no one else would have known. I still wanted out, so I reached tugging on my I.V. That same nurse bent down looking me in the eyes telling me she would hold my hand, and that I would be alright. I didn't want to close my eyes any more than I wanted her touching me. I've watched too many movies and heard too many horror stories. I didn't want to be another statistic.

I felt all of it was a setup. I was just home doing nothing, and that day was the complete opposite. The nurse grabbed my hand anyway, without my okay. I wanted to snatch it back and curse her out, but I didn't. I knew whatever was going on with my knee, was the reason I was in that situation in the first place. More tears fell as I slowly closed my eyes. I opened them immediately to look up one more time. Then I gave in. A mask was placed on the snout of my face. I took a deep breath as a natural response. My eyes opened, and I screamed. I squirmed on the hard bed, wanting the pain to stop. In a matter of seconds, it had gotten worse. The doctors and nurses ran toward me grabbing my arms and legs holding me down. I was punching and kicking the air. I heard voices asking what was I doing awake; it wasn't time. For some odd reason, I had awakened. I remembered nothing that happened after I was held down. But I knew I felt woozy and drifted off.

Joy M. Pierre

The next time I opened my eyes, the first thing I saw was a bright flashing light. It was painful to see, so I waited for my vision to adjust. It was the television. I twitched my nose and felt something in there. I raised my back trying to lift up but I couldn't move. It was my leg, with strange tubes hanging, so I panicked. I questioned myself why I had oxygen tubes in my nostrils. I looked to the left and the right side of me and no one was there. I pressed the call-light and my nurse came in. Many thoughts filled my mind, but the oxygen and the tubes were the first words that came out of my mouth. I knew I had surgery, and I also remembered waking before my time, but I didn't feel right. She reassured me to calm down, and that everything was okay. She told me when I was in surgery; I stopped breathing. My mouth dropped. And I looked down at my leg and then back to her. She continued talking telling me that after they stabilized me they took me to recovery because my stats were still low. I was puzzled as if she told me a story about someone else. I couldn't believe it. I cried, thanking the Lord for sparing my life. I was only 24 years old, and from the lack of understanding, juggling life was hard to cope with.

After being hospitalized for over a week, I was discharged with a PICC Line, an open line to my heart. Every time I looked down at my arm, the bruise constantly reminded me of what I was going through. I was a CNA so caring for myself was natural. But then, I was my own nurse, with an IV pole and dozens of liquid and pill medications. It embarrassed me to see myself handicapped. I knew others would laugh and humiliate me. I was ashamed, and my sister was all I had to depend on. Not meaning to take her for granted, I turned her home into my personal clinic, leaving little space for her.

While I stayed with her, it wasn't easy because it hindered the relationship between me and my son's dad. Our quality time together was limited since we didn't have a place of our own. An argument happened between me and my sister because of it. She was fed up and I had to get out. I thought leaving her house would help my son's dad become more responsible to care for me and our son. But I was mistaken. My journey was more painful. Not to mention how embarrassed I was, I wore a leg brace, and depended on crutches to move around, had a toddler to care for, and an IV pole and no money. I regretted leaving my sister's house.

As for my last resort, my uncle told me that things would get better. He offered to take us in, so we stayed with him a while. Guess who else came? We lived in the basement. Since I was on welfare, I used my food stamps to buy food for the house. I was glad my uncle took us in because I couldn't go back to that shelter. As a daily routine, we spent countless exhausting hours searching for homes. We called multiple landlords from the classified section of the newspaper.

I can remember spending many hours cramped up in the front seat, driving up and down the streets looking for rental homes. I filled out a lot of unnecessary applications and paid ridiculous fees, just to be ripped off. After a while, we found a home. The owner was moving to Lawrenceville, Georgia to start a new life. I moved in with the mindset of not failing because I wasn't stable before.

Chapter 2

All I saw was her feet. It was her soles to be exact. The image of what it looked like to carry a large load of hard work. There were more than just hers. The others were free from burdens. I thought to myself, how could this happen? She had a great personality and a smile to die for. As for the little one, my question was why?

My dad and his wife made choices that had torn us apart. She moved closer to Detroit, which was far. It seemed that everything in Flint was about 15 minutes away. Me on the other hand, that was the reason I moved out in the first place. I dealt with the real world my way. So did she but that wasn't her first time on her own. I made choices that lead to great responsibilities and she was supportive while she chose to take her own journey. She was the type that loved someone with every part of her soul. When she liked a guy she was really into them. She knew that marriage was a big part of her life and I did too. She stressed the importance. I wasn't thinking that far and all I cared about was me and my son. I did want the American dream one day, but at the time I could barely take care of myself.

Depression was my best buddy, and plus I was still dealing with issues from my surgery. My other sister was still mad at me from our fallout. I knew she hated me by then. One hot morning with birds chirping for an alarm clock made me fluff my pillow. My phone rang, I open my eyes in disgust and rolled over falling back asleep. The phone had rang again. That time I jumped up to see who it was. It was my sister, whose last word to me were get out. I stared at the phone long and hard letting it ring to catch the voicemail. It rang a third time and I answered saying what. She told me to calm down and that we were having a family meeting at our dad's house. I knew it had to be some baloney because none of us really communicated with him.

When I made it there I fell to my knees yelling as tears hit the paved sidewalk. I knew they had to be joking. At least they better had. That couldn't be true. She would never do such a thing. Many family members surrounded me lifting me from the ground. I knew at that moment I had lost my mind. It went blank and I couldn't think.

It all started back when my sister and I moved out of our dad's house. She knew that it wasn't going to be easy to work and take care of her child. She was in the process of finding a place for them to stay. She had a few good friends who lived in Detroit and in Pontiac, Michigan, where she worked. Plus, we had an aunt who lived in Detroit and who pretty much watched over us for some time after momma died. We thought of her as the meanest human being God could have created. But that was her way of showing us love and wanting the best for us,

Joy M. Pierre

knowing we had a void in our lives.

My sister found an apartment close to her job in Pontiac, MI. That's where she met a guy and got close to him. They worked together. She told me stories of how women used to be jealous of their relationship. He was well known and liked by many. On holidays, she would bring him to Flint to visit us. They were a nice couple. You could tell they enjoyed being around each other.

My sister was a clean freak with OCD. She kept her apartment clean, and no one was allowed to touch or rub against her walls. She planned to have more children, but after many attempts, she gave up. A few years later her dream came true and she was pregnant. We were happy for her and the addition to the family. We took a trip to Pontiac to her baby shower to support her. It was lots of fun. Her guy took his son and my nephew to the mall until the baby shower was over. They came back in time to help load the gifts she received. She had difficulties throughout her pregnancy with back, stomach pain, and foot swelling.

Her relationship issues peaked because she was on bed rest only receiving a percentage of her earnings. The bills fell behind. I knew she would get past it because she had a heart of steel and giving up wasn't an option. Back when I had knee surgery, she took my son to Pontiac with her because I needed help. I gave her the money I had, just in case she needed it. She kept him for a whole week and I didn't want to cause her any further financial hardship.

The day she went into labor was never forgotten. She yelled for help, my nephew didn't hear her. He must have thought he was dreaming. After multiple shouts, he jumped up to see what was wrong. She needed help. He called two people, but it was early in the morning and everyone was still asleep. He ran out the apartment door and hurtled up 20-30 steps to a neighbor, who lived a floor above them. He banged on the door until someone opened it. He blurted that his mom was having the baby and needed help. He rushed stumbling down the stairs to tell her help was on the way and to get her things.

There was still some good people in the world. Her neighbor drove them to the hospital. That day was emotional for her and everyone else. Many questions were asked. The whereabouts of my nephew and her guy, and how she and the baby was doing. I knew she was overwhelmed, but the worst she could have done was shut down on us. The same problems she had when she went to the hospital was waiting on her when she got out. Those same bills were still overdue. She was off work for six more weeks. My other sister and I still weren't talking. I'm guessing to see who could hold the longest grudge. My sister and the baby came to Flint to visit the family. She went over to my other sister's house and asked me to come too. I knew it was a setup and of course, I went along with the plan. She knew how I felt about my stubborn sister, and I didn't care to see her. I was upset and confused about why she chose to throw me out. I changed my mind and never made it.

She brought the baby to my uncle's house where I was. When I saw the baby, my eyes lit up, and I cooed. She was so cute with the chunkiest cheeks. The time we spent was good enough for me to lay eyes on the baby and smell her scent. My sister ended up having an eviction notice on her door when she made it home. As a natural response, she panicked. She asked her guy for help, and between the both of them, a payment was made. But, it wasn't enough to cover the payment in full. By that time, I

Joy M. Pierre

had moved into a new place. She asked me and my son to come down for a weekend and visit her church. She enjoyed church and continued to let the Lord be the leader of her life. She was very church-going and made sure she paid her tithes and offering. I went without hesitation. She was big sis. She picked me and my son up, and we hit the highway, going 80 miles per hour. She turned the blasting music down telling me that she was moving with her guy and he had found a place in Detroit.

She let me listen to a voicemail that he left for her. I heard him say that he was getting things together and that he didn't have a lot of spare time to stop by, and someone would drop money off to her. I asked her where the house in Detroit was. She mumbled a street name. I asked her to show me. She turned the music back up and we rode to Detroit. We were going to see the new place he picked out for them.

We drove up and down streets, getting lost. We didn't have fancy touch screen phone to use google maps or any other apps to guide us. It frustrated her, there was no house. Kids were running under open fire hydrants, staying cool. I looked over at her, knowing she wasn't about to do what I thought she was. She did. A big splash hit the windshield and water poured inside the truck. For the first time, I saw her act worry free. That was the total opposite of her norm. If you couldn't touch her walls, what made you think she would let water soak her cloth seats? I knew she was mad because I was. I told her to call him. She said he was at work and that she didn't want to bother him. Then I knew something was strange. There was no house and she didn't want to call him. Our journey back to her place was quiet. When we arrived, I saw her entire apartment boxed up. I was even madder. She was ready to move to a house her guy had promised, but it wasn't one. She had packed things up so tight that I had to search through boxes in ordinary to find a pot to cook.

Saturday morning, I saw her pick up a white envelope from the ground, near the front door. She opened it and it had cash in it. She said someone must have slipped it under the door. That was strange too. It was like she was being paid off to move on with life. Plus, the apartment security door didn't open unless someone let you in or if you held a master key. I was positive her guy had a key. He was the father of one of her children and her boyfriend. Thinking nothing, I figured it was him that slid the envelope under the door, because of the message she played for me.

On Sunday we went to church as planned. Lord knew I needed him, with that bad knee I had. She began to cry badly during service. It was a hard cry, and I was scared. That moment I knew something else was going on that she didn't mention. She walked up to the altar, where she cried more and asked for forgiveness. It was very touching. I cried too because I was sad and I thought back to Friday when we rode around not finding the house, and then the white envelope that was slid under the door.

I loved her and felt he was playing her, but only she was going to be able to determine her end to his lies. Her cries sent chills through my body. I used to get goosebumps. I didn't know or understand everything she went through, but the challenges we experienced was enough to make anyone cry. That weekend I was there, she did not talk to her guy once. I didn't say much because I didn't want things to upset her any more than she already was.

We left the church and got our things to return to Flint. I knew it had to be more to life, learning about my sisters' relationship. That couldn't have been the life she wanted or anyone else. Back at my place, I started a conversation by asking what she would do if her plan didn't work out. But all she said was move back to Flint. When she said that, I hoped things didn't work out so she would be close to me again. We both knew the hard part was getting out of Flint, but it was always easy for someone to come back. She left when she saw worry in my eyes.

I called her the next day, to see if she had new plans. I was hoping to hear her say she was moving back to Flint, but she answered the phone telling me she would call me back before I had a chance to say anything. While I waited for her to call me back, I was in deep thought. I wanted to hear from her because I didn't want her living out in the streets, and I knew that Friday was her moving day. I didn't hear from her that Tuesday, Wednesday, or Thursday.

That Friday morning was the day I lost my mind when my knees hit the ground. I looked through the crowd, up at my dad and got up rushing through them. I stood in front of my dad, looking into his eyes. There was nothing wrong with him, but he was a mental disaster. Someone kept blurting my sister and her baby's name. With my head lowered I heard others say they were in a house fire and were dead. That wasn't believable. I looked up at the crowd in denial. I broke down into tears again yelling and screaming. I was just down there with them. Many thoughts of her not being a smoker, and how she would never leave her electric stove on, was puzzling. I knew it couldn't be true, and it had to be a nightmare that I needed to wake up from.

My body became numb as family members tried to lift me from the ground again. I placed my hands over my eyes, hoping to end the nightmare. It didn't, so I screamed louder. I felt someone killed my sister and niece. Distraught wasn't a word for how I felt. I was irate. Our family was victims, and no one could convince me that her death was accidental. Our family took a ride to Pontiac in tears. It felt like an eternity to get there. I was confused. Something was wrong. She would have never set her own house on fire, nor would she forget the stove was on. It wasn't like her to do such a thing. That was the day she was supposed to move into her new place. Everything was packed and ready to go.

When we made it to the complex, her building was roped off with crime-scene tape. We got out the car walking toward the building and was stopped by officers and detectives at the scene. We told them we were family and they took us to the side and gave us updates. We were already informed it was a house fire, but we weren't aware that foul play was also a factor. Everyone cried and sobbed. We hugged one another to keep each other from falling to the ground. I yelled, I just saw her last weekend, and that none of it was true, and how she was fine when she dropped me off on Sunday.

One of the detectives took me to his undercover police car, where he questioned me. I asked where her boyfriend was. I asked if he could find him because I thought he was in too deep with some bad guys and they could have thought he was in the apartment with my sister. I gave him a long statement that was too hard to remember due to frustration. The bodies were already taken to the hospital to be examined before we arrived. We knew it would be a while or days for the autopsy report, so we waited for the coroner to call us. To pass time we headed to Detroit. Her son was over to our aunt's house. We drove away speechless from the painful scene. On our

Joy M. Pierre

way there, we received a phone call. Someone answered it and there was more crying. This was all too much to handle. We couldn't handle anymore. At that moment we were broken, and weren't expecting the results that were delivered to us. The foul play resulted that she was shot in the head, and then set on fire.

I knew she couldn't be the same person because she had no enemies; I thought. She always said her only enemy was the Devil himself. She was to giving to hate anyone. Most knew her as the church lady and I knew her as an evangelist. At my aunt's house, my dad went to the front porch and sat on the stairs, sighing, and waiting for my nephew to come out. He ran to my dad happy to see him and sat next to him not knowing what news awaited him. A tear fell from my dad's face as he told him the terrifying news. His scream was worse than ours and we all cried together. My dad explaining that his mom was never coming back and that he wouldn't be able to see her anymore.

That tugged my heart because he was only 10 years old, and it was awful to think of him having to grow up without his parents. Because momma left me at an early age too. I knew he didn't understand, but the day he missed her and knew she wouldn't come back would be his turning point. I knew he would be angry and torn from watching others enjoy their families, while he would see himself an outcast, out of confusion. I felt what happened to them and my nephew was overwhelming.

The news was depressing. They only blossomed crime. Their view was a killing and fire took place in Pontiac, MI. They told how a woman suffered severe trauma to the head at 31, and her daughter died from smoke inhalation at two months. They said her alarmed neighbors sobbed outside their doors and knew her as a shy and quiet person. That's all they said. That day was exhausting. They didn't understand the severity it caused us because it wasn't them facing the tragedy.

So I put all that confusion together. On the day of the tragedy, someone from the complex called 911 about 4 a.m. Friday after smelling smoke. The firefighters found two bodies in the bedroom after extinguishing the blaze. The police had no suspects, which made me more curious. Which was leading to an unsolved mystery. I wanted answers because that couldn't be true. I was torn up, first by the thought of someone hating her and my niece that much to kill them. Second, that someone was getting away with it. None of it was sitting right with me.

Detectives went to her guy's workplace asking him to come in for questioning. In the interrogation room, he spoke with a Detective. He asked him how to spell his daughter's name. Out of shock, her guy couldn't spell it. When the detective asked about his whereabouts on Friday, he stated that he was in many relationships with other women with whom he had fathered children. The detective told him about the deaths, and it surprised him that such a thing happened. That was the first time he had heard about it. He claimed the detective had to be joking and that it couldn't be true.

When the interview was over, he shook hands with the detective and agreed to take a polygraph test. He knew he had to clear his name because he wanted whoever committed the crime found. As nervous as he was to take the test by it being his first time, he was okay. The test came back inconclusive. After days of no witnesses and suspects irritated me. Someone still roamed the streets free. Days later her guy went back to the Pontiac

Joy M. Pierre

Police Department, wanting to help in the best way he could. He asked if they had any new leads. The detective reassured him they were doing their best and hadn't given up on the search. The detective told him they had a suspect in mind. Waiving his rights he told the detective he had been dishonest on his first visit.

It amazed the detective he came back to say such. He wasn't the suspect they had in mind. The detective asked him if he was sure and if someone sent him there. He told him he had come on his own. The detective asked if he had flipped out. His story changed again. He said he didn't do it. The detective asked him again if he had done it or not. His story changed again. He said he had been playing with the gun by spinning it in his hand while my sister was asleep. He said he didn't remember putting a bullet in the chamber, and that the gun accidentally discharged hitting her in the head. He claimed it all to be an accident.

All that was untrue. As madly as I was, I couldn't believe any of that. But I knew one thing, he couldn't spell his daughter's name, and he wanted nothing to do with her to begin with. I thought it surprised him to hear about the deaths, but he wasn't. He knew all along what had happened to my sister and his own baby. A quick run back was, he said he was spinning the gun in his hand and it went off. Who plays with a loaded gun? I didn't understand why his polygraph test was inconclusive; he must have been a great liar. I guess he waived his rights because he was haunted by what he did and knew he wouldn't get away with it. I knew he was the only one who had a key to her security door. He himself had to slip the money under the door. If he didn't want to be involved with her anymore, he should have left her alone. What bothered me was his attempt could have been to take her life that night I was there, but since me and my son were there, his plan wouldn't have worked.

As evidence kept unraveling, I felt he never intended to move her into a different home. Most of all to find out he was in relationships with other women, was plain pitiful. He even had a lady pregnant around the same time of my sister and their baby's deaths. I knew she had to be scared to hear what happened, because she could have been next.

He had to shoot her on Wednesday night, early Thursday morning while she slept next to their daughter. The same day he found time to visit other women to establish some kind of alibi. He took the lady who he had gotten pregnant to her doctor's appointment. After, he went to another lady's house where he took a nap. He still went to work, like nothing happened. And on his lunch break, he went to Meijer's to grab a T-shirt and jogging pants. No one suspected him purchasing clothes because wearing them weren't out of the ordinary. After work, he went back to the same Meijer's to buy gas. He paid for gasoline and put it in a gas can. He also bought a water bottle to place the gas into, so it wouldn't look suspicious when he went back to the apartment where she had been dead for many hours. As crazy as all this sound, he went back to the apartments bravely. He walked through the quiet house down a long hall to her room. He peeked in the room to see her still there. There was no turning back. He had to finish what he started. He walked in and flickered gas, allowing it to hit the walls and the bed, until more and more came out. He looked over at his daughter and begun to douse gasoline on her. She cried some, which startled him so he doused her and my sister and lit a match. He looked at the bright flame and tossed it to the bed. His daughter screamed at the top of her lungs as he ran out of the house. That part bothered me for years.

Joy M. Pierre

I blamed myself for not paying better attention to them. I knew it wasn't my fault, but I knew it could have been something I could have done to prevent it.

I was just there the weekend before, kept repeating in my mind. Even the thought that he left his baby all by herself. She was only two-months-old. I knew she heard the noise from the gunshot that pierced her eardrums. She had to be hungry and wet too. So all that time she was by herself, I knew she screamed for help until she cried herself to sleep. There was more to that vicious crime he committed. He also had no criminal history. When he confessed, he claimed that my sister had been cheating on him and had given him a sexually transmitted disease, which was a lie. I felt it was the other way around. He was the one living a lie, who had many other women. My sister was a good girl, and he knew it. He took advantage of her. He used her vulnerability to defeat her. The day we went to church, and she went to the altar crying badly, was the day she asked for forgiveness and the strength to leave her boyfriend. She knew he would not take part in the life she planned for them. She wanted and deserved more from her relationship.

His intentions were different from hers clearly. I was so confused that their six-year relationship could turn into such bitter outrage. I was sickened even more by all the truth. I couldn't eat or sleep. Every time I thought about it, I vomited or had diarrhea. After she died, I called her cell phone and pushed the code to her voice-mail many times. I heard multiple new messages that he had left after her death. He said he was calling to see if she was ready to move.

I couldn't believe my ears. He left another message telling her to pick up the phone and call him back. He had it all planned. He knew to cover his tracks by acting as if he didn't know where she was, or as if she had run out on him.

I became an alcoholic, thinking drinking would solve my problem. All it did was make me hate him even more for what he did to my family. My mind took over my body. I neglected my body by allowing the poison to take over my ego. It kept bothering me and I couldn't find a solution to stop the pain. I wanted someone or something to just carry me away from my misery. It shattered my composure to pieces like a broken mirror.

It felt like someone reached down my throat and pulled the life out of me. I felt as empty as a person stranded in a desert with a water bottle that had only one drop in it. I was also the river that broke through the dam, allowing my stream to get lost. I had no direction. The road I took was complicated for the bird's-eye view. That war wasn't a nightmare; it was existence.

They notified me from her apartment complex to pick up mementos and keepsakes. One of my uncles took me. When we got there, the door was unlocked. We walked in and saw that the house was in chaos. The firefighters put the fire out in two different places. I saw all the boxes still stacked up in the same fashion as when I had left her the weekend before. They had soot all over them. There was an odor of death in the apartment which made it impossible to stay there for a long time. It was a smell that made your nostrils flare. I walked to her room, where the smell was more powerful, and all I could say was oh my gosh. Her bed had burned to the floor, and they threw the mattress around. Blood was on the mattress and wall. The mattress tipped over, and I almost threw up. Beneath it was a pile of blood that had maggots crawling in it.

Joy M. Pierre

I knew it was time to go. I grabbed photos and keepsakes heading for the door. I looked around one more time to see how damaged the apartment was. It had not affected my nephew's room, but all his clothes smelled badly like smoke, and it would have took a long time to get that smell out, so I left them. We loaded things up and went back to Flint.

Days later I had a dream. She appeared in it and said she was okay and in a better place. She said the food was great; better than the food that anyone prepared for holidays. I kept telling her I wanted to see her more, and she said, "One day, you'll see me, and we will both eat together." She let me know she was in a better place and for me not to worry. It spooked me because she was sitting on the same couch in my house when she dropped me off after we got back from church that Sunday, and also the last day I saw her alive.

I got angrier. I wanted to kill him myself. I didn't want him to go to prison and live the rest of his life. For what? What was that going to prove? He took the lives of innocent people, not to mention people who were my loved ones. I felt his choices forced me to pick out a casket for them. I didn't want to be a part of that. Going to the graveyard was the hardest part, knowing we had buried them, not knowing if their bodies were actually present. It was so unfair. As usual, after funerals, everyone went their own separate ways. That was one time when life was priceless for me.

I felt disappointed when the time came for the preliminary hearings. The family members I thought needed to be there, wasn't. It killed me every time I had to walk in that courthouse without them by my side. I needed them with me. They were hurting, and I was too. I went to the hearings because I had to make sure my sister and niece didn't die in vain. I couldn't allow him the opportunity to be freed. I knew if I could handle it, they could too. But I have learned that we all grieve in different ways.

The judge knew how gruesome the evidence would be, he omitted the jury. The judge saved potential jurors from being exposed to the horrific scenes. It would have traumatized them. Everyone wasn't cut out for that type of exposure.

As I waited for the day to testify, it made me hysterical. I didn't know if he would send someone to hurt me, so I wouldn't testify against him. I wasn't sure what to expect. I knew the facts about what happened to them, so I was paranoid. I became more aware of my surroundings, by staring at everyone's features. I also gave them a second look to make sure they weren't following me. And I made it a priority to double check the doors and windows at my house and my car, every time I got in and out. I repeated it daily until the trial.

Once the day of the trial came, all my family made it to the Circuit Court with me. Despite their presents to support the case, mentally I wasn't ready. My body was trembling. I couldn't get my nerves under control, so I was biting the skin from my lips. I kept swallowing deep gulps because it felt like something clogged my throat. I wondered, how could I look at the man who killed my family?

I sat on a bench in a long, quiet hallway, waiting to be called to the stand. I wasn't allowed in the courtroom until I testified. I looked down at my hands and only saw a few hangnails, so I started picking, and biting them one by one. There were other trials going on and I saw others rushing in and out of the courtrooms. Every time the doors opened I looked in that direction, hoping it was my turn to testify, so it all would be over. But then again I was stuck in between. I had changed my mind about testifying, but it was too late to turn back. The long dreadful wait started playing tricks on my mind and I started hoping for a fight to break out in the courtroom. My mind was all over the place with all negative thoughts.

I was livid. So I waited... and waited... and waited, until the doors busted open. I stood up, and it was my family walking out of the courtroom. I ran over to them asking what happened. They said it was lunchtime and I would take the stand after recess was over. I had the most puzzled look on my face. I didn't want lunch. I wanted to know what really happened. It felt like they were hiding something from me.

I became more anxious and impatient, waiting for my turn. Then, my curiosity got the best of me, and I overcame my fear. I had to get inside that courtroom. I looked forward to seeing his reaction when I got on the stand. I wondered if he would keep his head lowered or raise it up to make eye contact. So, I walked back toward the courtroom pacing the floor waiting. My family walked up and went inside the courtroom. I stood still, eyes focused on them until the door closed, shutting me out. I sat back on the bench looking downwards with my hands crossed. I was moments away from my grand entrance.

The double doors opened. I jumped up. It was the prosecutor, peeking out the door calling me in with her hand jester. That was the moment I've been waiting for, but also, the moment of no return. I slowly walked into the courtroom. She quietly asked if I was ready while we walked toward the stand. Dozens of eyes were staring at me. I was telling myself not to cry until I finished speaking. I had valuable information about my sister's last days. I walked past the person who saw my sister and niece last. Like I expected, his head was lowered with his hands folded on the table. A bailiff swung open the door to the stand, and I walked in and took the oath, promising to tell the whole truth, and nothing but the truth, so help me God. I sat down in a narrow and hard chair. It was the most uncomfortable seat to sit in. And it was a place no one wanted to be in for a long length of time. Everyone in the courtroom focused their attention in my direction. I tried looking around, but I was focused on him. I knew everyone would be curious about what I had to say. So I said nothing. I wanted it to be the perfect moment.

My mind drifted off, and I jumped up from my chair and over the banister running toward him. He jumped from his chair. I charged towards him. In a blink of an eye, I hurtled over the table knocking him down. I stood over him like an angry bull striking a Matador. The guards rushed toward me so I reached my hands forward to strangle his neck.

Someone called my name. I snapped back to reality, forgetting where I was the entire time. Not realizing, my subconscious took over. I panicked, wanting to get down and walk away from it all. But there was no one else to take my place. It was like sitting in a hot spot. My palms felt like an inferno. I placed my hands on my knees, tapping my fingers against them. Not realizing, my foot was tapping the floor. I pushed my knees down to make them stop.

I was uncertain of what to expect. Gazing the courtroom, I shook my head trying to focus on the reason I was there. But I wondered if anyone else saw my out-of-body experience. The stare from the crowd answered my question. It was their interested look that made it more difficult for me to speak. No one knew what I would say, or if I would break down in tears. So they sat there in awe. My family members nodded their heads giving me the okay to speak because I had support. My limbs stiffened. It was a struggle to sit there. I cleared my throat realizing what he said, and I stated my name for the record.

The defense lawyer didn't take it easy on me. He asked me if I saw who slipped the money under the door, and all I could say was no. I felt it had to be him, but didn't know exactly who slipped it under there. So he asked me more questions that I could only answer no too. I was furious. He was trying to destroy me. I felt horrible that I didn't have proof. He snatched his chair out and sat down telling the judge no further questions as he rested his case. The prosecutor spoke soft asking me about a conversation I had with my sister the day we rode to Detroit searching for her unfound home.

I told how my sister was frustrated with him because she was days away from an eviction. And how she asked him for help because she knew he had the money, but refused to help her. She also said how he wasn't supporting her and my niece as promised. Then she mentioned how she would press child support on him if she had too. Then that's when she said something that stuck out from it all. She told me how it would make him mad if she did. I knew child support would make anyone mad, but I didn't know it would cost them their lives.

I was asked about her feelings toward him, which was easy. She was in love with him, doing anything in the world he asked. She also mentioned they would be married one day. And it was all interesting because he felt differently. I wondered if his plan was only to keep her content. Only 10 minutes on the stand for me, felt like a lifetime. Every time I answered a question I looked into the demon's eyes. He kept staring at me as if all the information I presented was new to him as if he never knew what happened.

The look on his face was as pleasant as if I was telling a story of someone else and not him. It was spooky. At times, while I was talking, he turned to his lawyer to whisper things. But I didn't care because everything I said was the truth. My emotions went from angry to panicking. I was waiting for him to jump up to say I was wrong. I kept watching him as he shook his head because I knew a lot of useful information he didn't think I knew. Then I thought again, he was mad that I was supposedly snitching on him. It was one thing to be a snitch by telling on someone just to better my chance of getting away with a deserved punishment. But that wasn't the case. There were two innocent lives taken, and I was defending my family.

After I finished testifying, more evidence was presented. I hurried to leave the stand and walk away. I sat in the courtroom next to my family watching him from the corner of my eye. The evidence of the case against left him defeated. He put his head down, and wasn't as tough as he put on. He was just like any other person that been caught in a wrong deed.

In the closing arguments, the defense attorney stated why he was innocent and should be freed with more jibber-jabber, just to be heard. He sat down and the prosecutor stood up. She identified him as a monster that committed a gruesome crime. She turned her back to the judge speaking to the crowd with a powerful tone. We all were crying. Pointing out the pain and agony we faced in the tragedy, was written all over our faces. She reminded us how he shot a mother, a sister, a friend, a daughter, and a woman of God. We sobbed even more. It was a terrible moment, but it had to happen. She pointed out how all his acts were premeditated, and he fully knew what he did. She even went further into detail with how he had a child from another woman, and had impregnated a third woman, and didn't want to pay support for my niece.

She stressed that after he shot my sister; he left to take his pregnant girlfriend to an appointment, went to work, then returned to my sister's apartment, where their baby laid screaming next to her dead mother. We cried even more because we knew where she was leading. She continued about an innocent life that didn't need to be taken. We roared when she said instead of taking the baby somewhere to save her, he deliberately walked over to her bed and doused the bed and them with gasoline. He heard the baby screaming louder, and he lit a match, throwing it on the bed to end it all. I lowered my head, placing it on my lap screaming. It muffled the sound, but it hurt too bad to pay attention to who heard me.

The Judge reminded us of the infant's pain. He stated how we would continue to hear those cries because my niece could have been saved. He told us that there was nothing more precious than life, the birth of a child, and how we should all love one another because it gave us hope for tomorrow. Even though he confessed to the killings, he had nothing to say to the court or us. He only shook his head when the judge asked for his last comments.

The judge found him guilty of two counts of first-degree murder, one account of felony murder, arson, and a felony firearm offense. Then the judge hit the sound block with his mallet. We were grateful as a family that justice was served, but it didn't take the pain away from having any closure. We hugged each other to walk out of the courtroom. Another lady stood outside the courtroom in denial. She was his other girlfriend, the one he kept a secret. She walked down the corridor and collapsed. He must have told her he was innocent, and she believed him. We waited for the prosecutor because she agreed to show photos of the scene after the case finished. She walked out of the courtroom and took us to a conference room. It was one large oval table with a dozen chairs. I pulled one out looking around. She opened the manila folder that carried papers and photos. She sat photos on the table one by one. The family cried and examined the photos. I sat patiently building myself up. I knew it was no turning back. I was warned the photos would be gruesome, but I had to complete that stage in my life. I still needed more closure. But finding out, still wouldn't give me what I needed. Apparently, I was the youngest, so I was last to see them. I didn't care about that; it gave me a better chance to see what I was in for. I saw different facial expressions of everyone before they reached me. I took a deep breath and sighed. Wow. She was right. It was horrendous.

My sister was on the bed. Her body was burned, but you could still identify the body. Maybe because I knew her. My niece's photo came, and I whimpered because I was still in shock over what he did to them. A strong burst of reality hit me. All I saw was pure innocence from the photos. My niece wore a pink jumper with teddy bears on it. I broke down mentally but didn't tell the family because they would have taken the photos from me. The rest of them were photos of the crime scene, but the photos of them were the main ones planted into my mind. After I saw the photos it changed the way I saw, did, and treated others. It altered my perspective on life and how I perceived others as well.

I wanted to get home to call my nephew to tell him the news, but it wasn't good news. He wasn't going to be happy either way. It still remains an unsolved mystery because I knew he would never tell the truth about what happened that day. That was one closure I said might never happen, so I left it there.

All of my hurt wasn't completely gone, of course. But, I knew at that point there was some purpose to everything that had been said and done. I had done my part, and I still chastised myself for all I could. I regretted not showing love to her every day and valuing her interest, and most of all support her dreams.

I still couldn't let it go. Every time I thought of mothers, sisters, Detroit, Pontiac, friends, fires, murders, babies, and him I got mad. He let his eyes control his every step. He had the audacity to commit one of the most horrendous crimes in the state of Michigan. Even though he was charged with life, I wasn't satisfied. Blood had flown through his body normally, and he had a continuous heartbeat, unlike my family. It may have looked like he was getting away with what he did, but he wasn't. I'm sure he was reminded every time he looked in the mirror of what he done.

On a routine, I searched the public record online to check his status. I looked at the photo of him and stared into the eyes of a murderer. I had recurring dreams that put fear into my heart. I was always in a two-story building that appeared to be home but didn't look like the current home I was living in at the time. People were chasing me with guns, and I didn't have a clue why. A man shot me in the head, and all I could see was a bright white light and heard a steady ring of a person in the hospital who just flat-lined. I was frightened.

I continued to have other, similar dreams. One time there were many men chasing me, shooting at me. The bullets were hitting me in the arms and legs to slow me down, so I couldn't run. I would wake, screaming and crying to the Lord asking for the forgiveness of all my sins. They had gotten worse. I didn't want to sleep at night for weeks. I wanted to stay up at night and sleep during the day. Night time was when I was haunted. I was on a praying spree. I prayed for healing, protection, and deliverance.

Shortly after that, my nephew came to visit me, he cried like a baby. It was nothing I could do but console him. I was hurting and missing his mom too. He reassured me he missed his mom, but that wasn't the problem. He told me he didn't want to go back to my brother's place. I talked things over with him, telling him things would be okay. He cried more suggesting to see his father. I told him how impossible it was because I had no information about him. It was years ago when they last saw each other. I remembered that his father paid child support, so since it was a weekday we drove down to the Friend of the Court in search of his father's information. I was hopeful to get a phone number or address for him. A lady asked us dozens of questions about why we were there. He cried and said he didn't want to live with my brother.

I looked at him and my mouth dropped. He tugged on her heart while she searched to find information. She stared at the computer screen teary-eyed, and told us she had a good friend he could talk to. Thinking nothing, I went along with it. That friend she had was Child Protective Services (CPS). They tricked me and things got out-of-hand. I sat nervously waiting because they spoke with him personally. He gave her a statement, and I had no clue what they talked about. I asked him when we left but they reassured me that someone was coming to my house to speak with us. I thought to myself, what happened in there? We made it back home, and a lady knocked at my door, and I let her in to speak with him. I remembered telling him to tell the truth and don't lie because someone could get in trouble for no reason. I sat listening to them talking back and forth with no interruptions. She asked if I knew a place suitable for him if he was to move from my brother's. I told her foster homes weren't an option. And if push came to shove, I'll move to a bigger home to keep him in the family until they found his dad. As a warning, she told me she was going over to my brother's house, and I knew it wasn't a good idea. I knew he would feel the situation was all my doing, which was wrongful thinking. My nephew cried for help and I remembered all the days I cried and didn't have an outlet. I asked the lady not to go over to my brother's; I didn't want to make trouble, but she insisted, telling me it was her job.

My brother called and said my nephew wasn't allowed at his house anymore. Then he asked if I was at home because he was dropping off his clothes. He said it so fast, I couldn't respond. The phone hung up and an hour later he was there with all my nephew belongings. I had no choice but to take him in. It caught me right in the middle. He had nowhere else to go. That brought major confusion between my brother and me. And it was already awful that I was hurting enough from losing my sister, so my other sister and him meant the world to me.

Days later he called me. He had paperwork for me to sign, but I was working. He agreed to come to my job so I could sign them. He called when he was near, so I took a break and went outside to his truck. I grabbed the handle and snatched it open. I wanted to talk to him and apologize. I leaned on the passenger seat and told him Hi and that I knew he was probably mad at me, but I didn't call CPS on him.

He shouted, so I backed up some. He told me he didn't believe me, just like I lied when I told him what my other sister's boyfriend did to me. Then he went on about how he found out we were messing around behind my sister's back. And how he still had the scars on him for taking up for me. I was shocked and hurt he felt I betrayed him. All that time, I thought he believed me and he didn't. I would have never messed around with my sister's boyfriend. I couldn't believe he attacked me like that so I stopped him in his tracks telling him I wasn't a liar, and I have nothing to lie about. Then I mentioned how I never lied to him and never would about something serious like that. He expected me to slam his door, so I did the opposite and shut it gently, remaining respectful.

After all of those years, I couldn't believe he thought I was a liar. I walked away in tears, back into the building, where a co-worker caught me. That situation had been serious, and it was heart-breaking he still didn't believe me. It was bad enough I blamed myself for years. Not to mention him and my dad carried scars. I felt nasty when it happened and a disgrace to everyone who knew the truth.

Chapter 3

Every time I looked at my nephew, I saw my brother's face telling me I was a liar. He was talking about the day I fell asleep on my sister couch. I didn't want to walk home in the dark. I would usually ask a friend to walk with me, but I didn't that time.

I was awakened by some pressure between my legs. His fingers were inside my panties. He must have been playing with me for a while, or he had some lubrication, so I wouldn't notice. I didn't have any idea because I was sleep and didn't know how long he had been there. When the pressure awoke me, I still had my eyes closed. You know how it is when you're lying on your stomach, and you wake up and turn your head from side to side but keep your eyes closed? It was like that. The only difference was that I was lying on my back, with my head turned toward the back of the couch. When I felt something moving in my panties to penetrate me, I moved my head slightly, thinking about what was going on. Next, I moved my legs as confirmation that someone was there, and he pulled his finger from beneath my panties and quietly moved away.

I heard him trying to tip-toe to the steps. The floor was squeaking. When he made it onto the steps, the steps creaked as he walked up the stairs. I could hear the floorboards squeaking overhead as he snuck into the bedroom and got into the bed with my sister. I could follow his tracks so clearly and hear his every move, because their bedroom was right above me. I knew it had been my sister's boyfriend by the way he walked.

I couldn't go back to sleep, because I was so uncomfortable; I couldn't believe what had happened. He violated me. I was ready to leave, but I wanted to make sure he was asleep first. I waited nervously for about twenty minutes. Then, I quietly got up and snuck out of the house, hardly opening the door, turning my body sideways to slip out. I shut the door behind me slowly, holding the door handle, so that the door wouldn't slam. I walked to a friend's house fast. I didn't want him to catch me leaving. I thought he might kill me if he caught me, and he wasn't a small guy. I was confused. I couldn't believe what had happened. He was like a brother to me. I didn't understand why he did that to me. I never thought that he would do something like that. He was nasty. Not to mention afterward, he didn't even wash his hands before jumping in the bed with my sister.

I made it to my friend's house and banged on the door, so I could get in the house quickly. His mom opened the door and let me in. She didn't question why I was there so early, and I didn't tell her. I went to his room to wake him up. I bent down on the bed and got into his face, whispering. He opened his eyes when he heard my

Joy M. Pierre

voice. I jumped back because I must have scared him. He yelled asking me what I was doing there.

He turned to look at his clock and said it's only a little after seven in the morning. I told him to stop speaking so loud. I whispered telling him I didn't want everyone to hear what I had to say. He quieted down blinking at me waiting for me to speak.

I looked him in the eyes as tears rolled down my face and blurted out that I was sleeping over my sister's house, and; I woke up, to her boyfriend's finger in my panties. He rose from the bed asking me what I said. I told him that he heard me and that he had his finger in my panties when I woke up. He jumped out of the bed and paced the floor, wanting to fight.

I got madder because he was making too much noise, so I left going down the stairs. I told him I was going home, and he told me to make sure I told my dad when I got there. On my way home, all that was running through my head was, how was I going to tell my dad what happened? I wasn't comfortable telling him that.

I made it home and quietly entered the house. I walked up fifteen steps slowly, feeling shameful. My brother was at home, and his bedroom door was opened, so I went inside and closed the door slowly, so it made no noise. I bent down in his face and told him to wake up shaking his shoulders. He woke up asking me what. I told him I had to tell him something. He got out the bed and sat on the edge asking me again to tell him what it was.

I stuttered, saying when I was over at our sister's house... I was sleeping on the couch. When I woke up, her boyfriend had his finger in my panties, while tears rolled down my cheek. My brother jumped up immediately, pacing the floor, putting on his clothes, socks, and shoes. When I saw him rushing, I asked him not to tell anyone. He told me he would not get away with it. I cried. I knew something was about to get ugly, but I didn't know what. He was slamming things around out of anger. He walked out of the bedroom and shouted at our dad. He opened his bedroom door and peeked his head out. My brother told him he's going to jump on my sister's boyfriend because he had violated me. My dad said I shouldn't have been over there, anyway, and my brother told him he was still going.

I didn't realize my dad was heartless. I couldn't figure why he would say that. I was heated. That was my sister's house. I had no idea he would have violated me like that. It wasn't my fault, was how I felt. I didn't give him any invitations. My brother ran down the stairs and out of the house slamming the door. I chased behind him. We jumped into the car and drove around the corner to our sister's house.

We opened the door and walked in. The house was silent. My brother rushed past me, running up the stairs shouting my sister's boyfriend's name. I turned and looked at the door because the screen door was hitting against the house because the spring was broken. By then her boyfriend had jumped out of bed and asked what's going on. My brother asked him what was up with him and me. All the time they were talking, I was standing on the stairs listening. I then heard feet tumbling. My brother punched him and they started fighting. They were wrestling bumping each other into the walls and punching.

My sister jumped up screaming, asking what was

going on. I ran up the stairs and over to her. I told her what happened, and she was shocked. My dad came out of nowhere and started punching too. The both of them were beating him up for what he has done to me. After they stopped. My dad, brother and I were leaving, and he yelled out that he didn't do anything to me and that I was lying. He was making everything he has done, a lie.

I couldn't believe what had happened. Everything was happening too fast. It all was like a recorder playing back repeatedly. First, I was violated. Then next my brother and dad were fighting him. We got back to the car, and my brother was silent. I was too afraid to ask him what he was thinking, so I said nothing. After we made it home, I was harassed by a phone call. I was told that I was a liar and how I liked him, and what he did to me was all a dream. Then, I was asked if we were messing around. I told them no, we weren't messing around, and what I looked like, messing with my sister's boyfriend. That wasn't me. I then cursed and hung up the phone. I couldn't believe they thought I was lying too. I was honest and it wasn't a lie. I wouldn't lie about something like that. Plus, I wasn't known for lying, so that helped my brother to know I was telling the truth, so I thought.

All of that was heartbreaking. I left the house and took a walk. I thought to myself that maybe I should have told no one. I knew what happened wasn't my fault; I did nothing to arouse his attention. Maybe my sister thought we were messing around too. That was my sister and I loved her, and I wouldn't have done anything like that to her or anyone else in my family. I understood karma.

I came home to a deserted house. No one was there. I knew they all were mad at me. Come to find out my brother and dad were at the hospital. My sister's boyfriend had come to the house with his homeboys to retaliate. One of them pulled out a gun shooting at our house. My nephew was on the porch and the bullet was heading toward his chest. My dad jumped in front to shield him and was struck in the leg by the bullet.

My sister's boyfriend ran toward my brother picking up where they left off, from the fight. He pulled a knife on my brother, and they tussled more. I know my brother didn't see that coming. He stabbed my brother all over, trying to kill him. My brother turned the knife back on him, stabbing him too. They both were in bad shape. They were taken to Hurley Medical Center for treatment. Hospital drama was never better. They separated families to hold down confrontation. My brother and dad were on the same floor in the hospital but only my brother was in the Intensive Care Unit. He was in the worst shape of them all. The boyfriend was on a different floor. No one knew where I was. But I knew if I was there I would have been a part of it too. My family didn't know if they had got me on the way to the house.

Ashamed to be seen, I didn't want to go to the hospital. I pulled myself together and went, anyway. I had to make sure my family was okay because all of that had taken place from what happened to me. I went to see my dad first. I walked into the room; it was crowded with family members. I said hello to everyone in a voice that made them sadder. They were glad I was okay but everyone knew they were in the hospital because of what happened to me. Family members hugged me as I walked past them to get to my dad. When I looked at him, my eyes watered. I said to him; I love you, and I'm sorry. My dad told me not to cry, and that he loved me too. We rarely passed the love word around so it was awkward hearing him say it. I told him I was going to check on my brother

Joy M. Pierre

and left the room. As soon as I made it to the hall, I felt a release of energy. I wondered if my family was talking about me, and not in a good way. It was only my word again his. They didn't know what to believe. I walked slowly to the ICU by myself. My brother had to have been in a serious condition to be in there. More tears fell, and I was so heartbroken and mad that all that happened. Down deep in my heart I didn't want to go see him, but I had too he stood up for me. I walked through the double doors and sobbed harder. I knew all that was my fault, and I blamed myself even though I was told I did the right thing. I thought if I had kept my big mouth shut, none of that would have happened.

I made it to his room and oh my gosh. I saw fleshy meat hanging from his body. I couldn't believe my eyes. Many machines were hooked to him with strange beeping. I was devastated. I walked to the bed and told him; I loved him and that I was sorry he was in there. I didn't know if he heard me or not because his eyes were closed, and he didn't respond. I pulled up a chair and sat by the head of the bed for a while thinking, Lord what have I done to my family? I claimed I loved them so much, and yet all these bad things had happened. They were just standing up for me. I didn't see anything wrong with that.

The only problem was my sister's boyfriend knew what he did to me and tried to clean it up by retaliating. I prayed more saying, Lord if they hadn't done anything about what happened, what would have happened to me then, nothing? My head was already screwed up, and I questioned why it happened to me. My sister didn't come to see my brother and my dad while I was there. She was with her boyfriend and his family. That made me believe she thought I was lying, and she believed whatever he told her. He acted without thinking because if he had thought about it for even a minute; he would have known what he had done to my sister, brother, dad, and me. He broke the family apart, and we let him.

My sister probably didn't think I was lying. She probably didn't know how or what to think. It put her in the middle of everything because of what happened. Even though she had to choose, it was her choice, and I still loved her. I couldn't be around to look her in the face, knowing she didn't believe me. I knew she wanted to continue to be in the relationship with him because she was in love.

My dad never pressed charges on him. Which also made me feel he was intimidated or believed him too. The boyfriend didn't get in trouble for what he and his friends did. My dad probably just wanted everything to be over. I was even more embarrassed when I watched the local news about what happened.

My dad got well enough to go home. As for my brother, he was still in recovery, getting better. I thanked God, but I didn't feel any better.

My sister and I haven't spoken for a good while after all that happened. I missed her company and wanted to see her and my nieces. Her youngest daughter was having a birthday party at Chucky Cheese and she invited me. I was undecided on whether I was going or not. But after realizing our side of the family wasn't supportive, I went anyway. Naturally, her boyfriend was there. I still couldn't stand to look at him. He always looked at me as if nothing ever happened. I stood at the coin machine to get tokens and saw him from the peripheral vision walking toward me and I was shocked. He spoke, and it surprised me. I was standing alone, and he blurted that he was sorry for what happened. I looked at him strangely. We weren't cool, and I knew any day forward we wouldn't be either. I knew exactly what he was talking about. What else would he walk up and say he was sorry for? I said the first thing that came to my mind. I told him I'm not thinking about that anymore and raced away. All that was running through my head was that he admitted to what he did and I had to hurry and get away from him.

I realized that he could have killed my family. And from all the trauma we faced, we still have the scars whether or not they're visual. I forgave him but I didn't forget the emotional burdens it caused me on how I handle situations today.

Chapter 4

My brother told me he sat reading the Bible in the living room when a shadow walked past him going up the stairs to where my dad was. He jumped up, Bible in hand, running to the bottom of the stairs, yelling my dad's name. He ran toward my brother's voice and shouted, what's wrong. My brother saw his face and felt relieved and responded by saying never mind. As he walked away, he knew his mind wasn't playing tricks on him. He looked back and glanced at the steps while he prayed hugging the Bible. But knowing he saw something put a shiver down my spine. I looked at him and bucked my eyes, wanting to tell him I saw things too.

Momma told us something was going on in the house, but we didn't believe her. She was a serious person and didn't play. She was the one you didn't want to cross. At the same token, she had good days too. She watched "I Dream of Jeannie," laughing and twitching her nose like a witch. On Saturdays, she jammed to "Soul Train," waiting on the Soul Train Line Dance to form. As she mimicked the dancers; she waved her hands and hips, clapping to the beats.

I never worried about momma because I knew she could hold her own. So when she did things I never questioned them. I felt she had her reasons. The day she told me people were watching her, and police in unmarked cars were following her too, I didn't find it funny. But that was the first, I've heard her speak such insanity. She was tripping me out.

One day I was riding with momma, listening to the radio. The radio cut off and the car died. A truck honked the horn from behind, startling momma. She jumped and tried to crank the car. It started, and she revved the engine, and shifted the gear to drive, the car clunked off again. Momma panicked. I looked at her with a confused look on my face. That wasn't the first time our car did that. The truck went around, and I thought the driver was mad and didn't want to wait for our car to start. The car stalled again. Out of frustration momma yelled, they're trying to kill us. It made me concentrate on her more. She kept repeating it and it made me scared. I didn't understand why she said that. I never heard her talk like that or seen her irritated. That was totally out of her norm. It felt weird. She tried to crank the car again, and it started. Momma pressed the accelerator so hard that the car jerked as it took off.

The entire ride home, I was nervous because of the way she was acting. I kept looking over at her, wishing I knew what she was thinking because I had no clue. When we made it home, I jumped out of the car slamming the door. I ran into the house to have a hushed conversation with my sisters. Their eyes squinted letting me know

Joy M. Pierre

they knew nothing of what she was going through. They also wondered what was wrong. Days later, momma over-protected us for no reason, and made us stay in the house to keep a close eye on us.

She had problems with stores and not only did I experience a situation, but my sister did too. The next time she went, she took my sister. They walked up and down the aisles shopping like any other day. Momma felt someone following her. She turned to look. It was a strange lady grabbing groceries from the shelves. Momma hurried to the next aisle. She dared to look behind her, not intending to see anyone. She turned back and gripped the grocery cart handle. Her eyes bucked from fright thinking she saw the boogie man. She took a deep breath balling one of her hands into a fist watching the lady walk toward her, hoping she didn't have to use it. Her personality wouldn't let her close her eyes, but her constant blinking got the best of her. She knew if she focused, she could make sure it was a person and not her mind playing tricks on her. She stumbled forward slowly, fighting her every step. Her heart pounded faster and faster the closer they walked toward one another. The lady looked up starring momma in the eyes. Momma's palms were sweating, so she snatched her palms from the handle of the cart and rubbed them on her pants legs. She grabbed a can of beans from the cart and wrapped her fist around it to use as a weapon. The lady was still looking in momma's eyes with a smirk. Momma was even more offended. The lady pushed her loud cart, rushing past momma grabbing items from the top-shelf. Momma tossed the can back into the cart and gripped the handle of the shopping cart shaking her head. She headed to the checkout lanes, shoving cash into the cashier's hand. Then she rushed the cashier for her change, so she could leave. My sister asked what was wrong, but momma ignored her and rushed to the car. The cart hit the bumper of the car. She threw the groceries in the trunk yelling at my sister in a panicked tone, telling her to get in the car. But my sister still walked at her same pace which was slow because she was mad.

Momma slammed the trunk running to the driver door, pulling it open. The door slammed, and she scrambled for the ignition key to crank the car. Her shaky hands struggled to put the key in the ignition. She cranked the car and sped off like a bat flying out of Hell. She looked in her mirror, and couldn't believe what she saw, so she slammed on the brakes to slow the car down, jerking the car. It was the lady from the grocery store behind her. The lady swerved around to avoid a car accident, and momma got mad all over again thinking she was trying to hit her. She squinted her eyes and jumped in the lane behind her. They passed many stop lights and street signs on multiple streets. The lady turned up a side street and drove up a long driveway, looking in her rear-view mirror. Momma pulled in behind her, so the lady jumped out holding grocery bags in her hands looking to see if she recognized momma's car. Momma jumped out too, while the lady asked who she was looking for. Momma busted out saying, she knew what was going on, and started an argument. The lady told her that she lived there. But momma still didn't believe her walking forward to argue more. Momma told her she was lying and that she didn't live there. Anger made her face knot up in a frown; she wanted to fight.

My sister pulled and tugged on her arm trying to get her back to the car. But the force of hell was with momma. She spun around getting loose. No one was there to help so giving up wasn't an option. Momma's angry red eyes glared at my sister. It was the look she saw many

Joy M. Pierre

times. And her insulting words were the same as the words she called us when we were in trouble. My sister grabbed momma anyway, and momma waved her fist in her face. My sister was scared but determination kept her going. The lady stood ready to swing her bags at momma's face. The closer momma came, the tighter she gripped the handles waiting on momma to swing first. My sister told momma lets go pulling and yanking on her shirt. Momma didn't realize the force my sister had, because she was back in the car gasping for air and rocking. Her lips were moving but nothing was coming out. She leaned forward raising her fist and pounded down onto the steering wheel. My sister fussed walking to the passenger side and hopped in ignoring her, because she was mad. Momma had embarrassed her by losing control.

When they made it home my sister told me about momma's behavior. I was worried about her. I never saw her act like that. Momma was doing other strange things too. So we could only imagine how her night was. Every door in the entire house was locked; the curtains were closed; things were out of place. They were the complete opposite of how momma did things. I looked at momma and she had big bags under her eyes. I didn't know if she had no sleep, or if she had been crying. My dad wasn't there, he was at work. So I helped momma by opening the doors and curtains and straightened up a little, so he wouldn't notice. Momma had also let her personal hygiene go. She stopped bathing, changing her clothes, and brushing her teeth. She was a chain-smoker that loved Kool Mild cigarettes.

One day in an effort to get momma to quit smoking, I hid her cigarettes in our living room's closet. Momma looked for them and couldn't find them. Her nerves got bad, so she went to the store and bought more. When she made it home, I let her smoke about three to four cigarettes, then I hid that pack too. Momma thought that she was really going crazy. She thought that she had smoked the whole pack. I continued to take momma's cigarettes for a whole week. Momma searched the whole house. I had an idea and knew what she was looking for. Momma made it to the closet door. My eyes bulged out. She put her hand on the door handle and I opened my mouth like wow. She pulled the handle, jerking the door open. All the cigarettes that I had hidden from her tumbled out. I didn't realize how many packs I had taken from her. It had to be over twenty packs. Momma yelled at me, asking if I had put her smokes there. Of course, I changed my facial expression and lied. She told me that someone had to put them there and I told her I didn't know who did it but I would find out for her. If momma had found out that I took her smokes, she probably would have smoked me. That was one thing she didn't play about. I kept the cigarette thief's identity a secret and she never found out. I wasn't going to tell on myself.

Another day, my dad asked momma to stop carrying her handgun. Previously, he saw her carrying it in a brown paper bag along with a bottle of red wine. Momma loved her red wine. Wild Iris Rose to be exact. Even my dad couldn't tell her anything. He knew momma thought people were after her, but he didn't know who.

He started to believe she was crazy. So he didn't pay her any attention when she acted out. He knew about all the things she done and didn't care. They didn't spend a lot of time together. They had grown further and further apart. I didn't know what to think so I thought she was mad at him and it was the reason for her behavior. I didn't have a clue what was really going on. I just sat back and kept my ears and eyes open. Days passed, and she was doing some of the same things, like carrying the gun in that brown paper bag again. My brother was helping momma to get out the house for fresh air. He had convinced her to take a ride with him. She looked out the window and told him to look too, and she said they were out there waiting for her. He looked out the window and told momma he didn't see anyone. She trusted my brother plus he was her firstborn. She agreed to go since he said everything was okay. My sisters and I jumped in the car too. We rode for a little while and ended up at McLaren Hospital in the emergency room. Momma wanted to know who had died and why we were there. She wanted to leave right away because she knew something wasn't right and figured we were up to something. We told her that she should check herself in so that she could see what was going on with herself.

We couldn't force her. She had to check herself in, on her own. It had to be something that she wanted to do for herself. We thought momma needed psychiatric help, so we tried our hardest to get her the help she needed. Momma had to sign her own paperwork but didn't do it. So she put the pen in her hand, got up and ran out the door through the hospital, trying to get away from us. We were surprised to see momma move so fast. She wasn't a small woman. Out of shock, we didn't move when she did so we ended up losing the direction she ran. Then we saw her, tip-toeing from one side of the hall to the other. We yelled telling her to come back, but that wasn't good enough. She was trying to find the exit, but the security guard caught her and walked her back to us.

She didn't want to be there. Trying to convince momma was a hard thing to do. All we wanted was for her to stay a while to see if things would get better. We just wanted the best for her. We loved momma, and we just wanted things to get back to how they used to be. Then my dad showed up. The words that came out of her mouth were she hated us and she would have never treated us like that. She said we turned our back on her and that she would never forgive us. We thought those were some harsh words and none of that was true. All we wanted was for momma to get some help. Momma signed the paperwork and threw the ink pen against the wall.

A few days of momma being gone, I was missing her and wanted her to come home, but I knew she needed help. I went to see her on visitation day. Even though I hated seeing her that way, I couldn't help but knock her over when I hugged her. My eyes watered and I tried holding back my tears because I couldn't let her see the hurt and pain I was suffering. I let her go. She saw tears on my face as I tried my hardest to hold them back. I only stayed for a bit because my dad didn't want me seeing her like that. I looked back at her as she watched us walk away.

For the first time, momma looked good. I hoped she looked even better when I saw her again, because she had another week there. The day she came home, I was happy she was fixed. I knew fixing her could put everything back to normal. She didn't waste time getting settled back in. She put on her routine house clothes and chilled. Out of curiosity, she dug in the drawers and the closets. I asked momma what she was looking for and she told me her guns. When they weren't where she put them, she ransacked the house until she found the guns that my dad hid. She needed them just in case. I didn't know what her plans with them were, so I didn't worry. The only thing that mattered was, she was at home. After being stuck in the house she wanted to get out more. She went to visit people she knew of but didn't know personally. I said to myself the hospital must have worked, be-

Joy M. Pierre

cause she wasn't a friendly person. Even the thought of her visiting our friend's parents was a major change.

One day, I wanted to stay the night with my sister over at her friend Will's house. Another guy, who liked me lived over there too. I really wanted to go because I liked him back. I begged momma to let me go, but she told me no. I begged and begged until she told me yes, and to get out her face. I left the part out about the guy because I knew she wasn't having that. I met up with the guy and watched movies, played games, and had good conversation. I guess because it was getting late he wanted more, on a higher level. We were young, so I didn't want to have sex with him. Not that I didn't know about sex; it's just that I didn't like him like that. I only thought he was cute. Then, he rubbed my leg and kissed me, but a bad odor from his breath turned me off. As any guy would, he got mad because I didn't give in. I wanted to go to sleep early because I didn't care if he didn't want to talk to me anymore; the next day was Labor Day.

Morning came, and we returned home to get ready for grandma's house. Our other sister told us that momma didn't get any sleep last night, and was shooting in the house. I was surprised to hear that. I asked her if she was shooting at our dad and she said no, she was in the kitchen. None of that made any sense. I shook my head because I didn't want to believe what she said. I walked away and they continued talking.

I wondered what she did on holidays, all by herself. Me and the rest of the family left around noon and didn't return until late evenings. So, I went to the mirror and took my ponytail out. Momma was in the kitchen getting bottles together to take to the store. I asked her if I could go with her as usual, but that time she yelled no. Something was wrong with her so I kept talking to her. I asked her why was she, taking bottles to the store when she had money. She yelled again telling me, because she wanted to. I wondered what was wrong with momma. She always took me with her. I thought what made that day different from the others. I looked around the kitchen somewhat believing what my sister said. Momma stood up and I saw a bullet hole in the bottom cabinet, which she tried to hide. My sisters were watching a couple arguing and fighting on "The Jerry Springer Show." While my dad was in the bathroom trimming his beard and mustache with loud overpowering clippers. I walked to the bottom of the steps and called his name grabbing his attention. He shut them off, and I told him that something was wrong with momma and not to let her go to the store by herself. He shouted back telling me she was a grown lady, and she could do whatever she wanted, while turning the clippers back on to finish. I stomped away. That was his wife for crying out loud. And it was a bullet hole in the kitchen cabinet. Something wasn't right. He was getting cleaned cut and handsome to leave momma at home, with the bullet hole she created, not knowing how many more would be there when we got back. I tried to blow it off, I wasn't messing up my Labor Day. I heard the back door slam as momma walked out. My sisters were still sniggling and laughing from the show when I walked past them, toward the kitchen. I dug in a drawer and pulled out a pressing comb placing it on the stovetop. I stood there for a minute or two waiting. My eyes wandered in the kitchen remembering what she supposedly did. Then it was confirmation she was shooting in the house. The bullet hole was weird. Momma was right-handed, but the bullet hole was on a left-handed angle. Looking at the hole trying to imagine what happened, I forgot the comb on the stove, so I snatched it. It was too hot to put on my hair, so I blew the smoke and walked back to the living room mirror.

Not meaning to pay attention to outside, I heard an ambulance siren coming down the street. We lived only blocks away from the hospital, so we heard them all the time. In less than five minutes, I heard a car pull into the driveway, and a car door slam. About a minute or two past and no one walked into the house, which was strange. I stood looking in the mirror for several seconds thinking, something was wrong. I walked back toward the kitchen to put the comb back on the stove. I made it through the dining room to the kitchen door and heard a loud gunshot. I paused because my brain had to register where it came from because it was only feet away. I yelled momma's name, throwing the comb, running past the stove, to the back door. She was laying on the back porch on her stomach. I was in shock holding my mouth screaming. My sister and dad ran past me pushing me out the way to get to her. My dad fell to his knees rolling her over. He pushed the gun away and cuffed her in his arms. I never saw my dad cry. His eyes were bloodshot red yelling her name and shouting get help. I stood there, feet heavy like the world had caved in on me. I kept looking, watching her eyes roll behind her head, not believing what had happened. He kept yelling asking her why she did it, but she didn't respond. Tears kept falling from his face onto momma. From rocking and hugging her, blood was all over surrounding them. One of my sisters were standing over my dad screaming and crying and my other sister was standing behind me crying too, saying come on let's get help. Momma was dying and I was watching it. I couldn't move until she pulled on my shirt, pulling me away.

We left running to get help. Since we had no house phone, our only option was to run around the corner to a friend's, to call 911. My mind kept flashing back to momma's orange, blue, and white vertical-striped shirt with her off-blue pants. We ran up the stairs and banged on the door. The door swung opened and we forced our way in, breathless shouting momma needed help. They didn't understand what we were saying so we tried to catch our breath and speak clearly. I was too emotional to explain what happened. I took a deep breath and shouted momma needed help. We blurted that momma had shot herself and we needed help. Our friend's dad and my sister ran back around the corner to the house. I wanted to go back too but I couldn't because I was told to stay. My friend's mom walked to the back room and I jetted out of the front door pushing the screen door open, flying home. Momma's face kept flashing before my eyes, I kept wondering if she okay? I had to see her. I knew some of that was my fault because I should have went to the store with her, after she told me no.

I made it home, the police and the ambulance were there. I saw EMS pushing a body on a stretcher, covered up with a white sheet. I tried running toward her but my sister yanked me back. Everyone on the block was there seeing what happened. All I kept hearing was I'm sorry. I looked around as the crowd whimpered I fell to the ground screaming. It felt as if every drop of blood in my body had rushed toward my head. It was pounding as if I was struck by a bulldozer. And a numb feeling of emptiness, had taken over my body. I didn't have a chance to give her a kiss, a hug, or even tell her how much I loved her. I was in denial and I wanted nothing to do or say to anybody. I just wanted to be alone. I heard voices in the background yelling and crying that she was gone. Everyone was in shock. None of us never believed she was capable of taking her life. I didn't know how I was going to move on. Momma had left us with our dad who was a stranger to us. He lived with us physically but had his own life outside our family.

He was the type that left home early mornings for work, come home, only to spend time in his own world. He loved the garage atmosphere so much that he made it his paradise. I wondered who would take care of me. How was I going to make it to the grocery stores? Who would make sure I made it to school and doctors' appointments? Who was going to nurture me to good health when I got sick? Momma was my pillar, my best friend, now she's gone forever. I was forced to grow up in order to take care of myself. She left me defenseless to care, think, act and take on adult's responsibilities all at the age of 13 years old. She was 40 the last time I saw her. I couldn't imagine walking in her shoes knowing I'm getting close to reaching her age. I was terrified by those bad behaviors and mood swings I've described; she suffered from Paranoid schizophrenia. The Medical Examiner did not explain to us in simple terms of what that meant, but I knew to call other's schizo's meant they were crazy.

I still couldn't believe she took the easy way out. I thought she was just angry with life. Momma's parents weren't around either. I never met my grandma, she passed away before I was born. Momma never mentioned her other than that. But I met my grandad, and he was anything but nice. I can remember him coming over to check on us, from time to time. Every time he came over he would reach into his pocket and pulled out hands full of change and separated between the four of us. As for momma, he was always mean toward her, cracking jokes. His favorite saying was, dang girl you still eating all the food from the kids? I never found that funny. She was a tall big-boned lady. Yes, she did put on some weight from having us, but it gave him no rights to degrade her in that matter. They hated each other, and momma couldn't stand to be around him.

Sadly, the old man passed away sitting on the toilet from a heart attack. Momma was in a state of madness for a long time after his death. She lashed out lots of anger that was buried from deep within her heart. Not because she lost my grandad, but because she wanted revenge. She told me how she was counterplotting on killing him herself because of the stories she told me about how he used to molest her when she was young. It was so bad that she ran away from home, and lived in the streets. Her only survival tactics were to eat out of dumpsters. I saw tears fall while she stared off to the side of the room. She also told me she had another daughter before me who died in a house fire. She thought to have more kids was a thing of the past. But once the incident happened, I came along. It wasn't easy for me to grasp it all. I even felt bad because I wouldn't have been here. I was an afterthought. If I was only conceived because they chose to have another child to replace her, how in the world was I born 4-months after her death? Did she know she was pregnant? Was I born premature, and no one told me? Was she losing her mind then?

It was a heartbreaking feeling. I felt jealous behind it all. I hated stories about my family when I wasn't born. Then, they talked as if they wanted her around instead of me. It was nothing personal against her. I never met her. It was those same constant reminders, that I wasn't born yet, that killed me. Not realizing, I was childish for being jealous of a sister I never met. She could have been that same sister that brought inspiration into my life. She could have been that push I needed to get back on track when I was in need of direction.

My low self-esteem formed a long time ago from

momma's depression days, and I didn't realize. When she was happy I was happy, and when she was sad I was sad. Her moods worn on me. She was miserable more than content with her life because she felt alone. With no parents, we were all she had to hold on to. My dad spent no quality time with her, which was sad. She was beautiful and done the best she could by taking care of us. In life, I've learned that you only function on things you're taught. She had no role models and wasn't taught anything but to defend and protect herself. There were no sparks in their marriage. So I knew marriage would have been a challenge for me too. I knew I would have those times when I wanted to give up because giving up was always easy to do. It's the moving forward part in life that everyone was afraid of. I called it the unknown. While we thought the best things in life was to live with your family in the same house. We mastered it, but yet lived so far apart. We were living in two different galaxies.

Momma and my dad had issues a long time ago. By being young and sensitive, I believed that they had the perfect relationship. All those nights they slept in the same bed with their backs turned, didn't help either. But seeing them sleep in the same bed was what I expected love to look like. I never understood why momma told me it took a long time before she spoke with him again. She used to always talk about a fire that happened before I was born. Growing up every time someone asked how many siblings I had, I thought of the sister and that puzzled story. The more I thought and wonder about what could have happened, compelled me to dig for the truth.

I went to The Flint Journal snooping around for hours searching archives for information about my family. All the broken pieces momma told me about made me wonder on a deeper level. I saw a small, disappointing article with my dad on the front page with his arm wrapped in a bandage. Even though the photo was taken at an angle, you could see the full expression of defeat on his face. His photo was larger than the article itself. I thought I would see more on the story because losing a child is a big deal. But I was wrong. All I found was a one paragraph article that gave me more questions than answers.

I read that an 11-month-old was killed in a house fire when the pilot light ignited from gasoline fumes. My dad told investigators that he filled his scooter with gasoline in the basement at his supposed ex-wife's home.

It devastated me. They were supposed to have been married or were they divorced and we didn't know. I remembered her words; she thought he had the baby and vice versa. He tried running back in to get her, but the sizzling heat and black smoke spread instantaneously. She said she kept screaming, that her little girl was in there after realizing the rest of the kids were across the street playing and my dad didn't have her in his arms. I still remembered the look on her face as a tear fell from her eye, while she looked downwards at the floor. Momma had the look like she wished it was her in the fire instead. I knew it was a hysterical moment to see the blaze destroying her life, all in a split second.

She continued the story saying my dad rushed back towards the house rescuing her, but the hot fiery blaze pushed him back. While she paced the pavement screaming looking toward the house, my dad was coughing and gagging from the thick smoke. Even though she said she didn't want him running back into the house, it left him no choice. Their daughter was inside and he wanted to save her. As she was talking, she lifted her head and frowned her face. Her tone switched from sadness to anger. She stared in the days like she wanted a peace of mind. When she told me about the tragedy, she hadn't realized she was reliving the moment. Her face alone told the story but her voice carried out her actions.

It was painful to believe the story was true. But the way she talked about it, convinced me that something went terribly wrong.

It was no way that the fire should have started from just the pilot light ignited and gasoline fumes. Something had to spark to create a combustion. Yes, he had gasoline as a fuel. And I could understand that we breathe air that produced oxygen. But what I didn't understand was, how a house fire starts without something creating a spark? From one of my science classes, I was taught that you needed oxygen, fuel, and a spark. But without all three there should have been no combustion.

Momma told me my sisters and brother were outside playing before it started. When they saw them both running out of the house and down the steps yelling fire, it scared them. So I knew they had nothing to do with starting the fire. As for my dad, momma said he only suffered cuts and no burns. Which was hard to believe because it was a fire. Her last words were they stopped talking to each other for a while because she blamed him for it all.

There was no way I could relate to her experience of losing a child. But I knew it had to be devastating. And the fact of living with the shame of who was at fault didn't make the situation better. I realized now that could have been one of the reasons they were so disconnected.

I'm sure they had no clue they were dysfunctional. Many used the saying, I'm doing what I have too, just to get by. I'm sure we all used that saying at least once in our lifetime. Excuse free, we sometimes follow our parents' footsteps. And if their parents abused or neglected them, they're likely to abuse their children or are extremely lenient in letting them get away with bad behavior. But it shouldn't matter how dysfunctional you are, it still didn't condone or explain the truth to the fire.

My feelings about the house fire were like a grenade that went off and shattered the family relationship. And it had a major impact on how we grew up. Our family time was rare as if they just gave up on life. There was no respect for one another and they set no boundaries in the household. At first, it didn't bother me that my dad had his own personal life while momma was always home doing her own things. But then again, I only thought they had gone through petty situations and nothing serious. Growing up, all of it was important to me. I wondered what it felt like to be supported and encouraged by loved ones. I can say my parents never explained anything from the golden book of life. But the more I observed them, determined if my adulthood would have been a reflection of their life. I wondered if counseling would have helped me with the reasoning of my family behaviors. But I felt counseling would only comfort me with accepting who they were. Momma had a way of instilling fear in us. She constantly reminded us that she was all we need. And her favorite saying was, she brought us into world and would take us out. We had no choice but to believe her.

So I flashback about the day when momma was yelling at my sister, for inviting her friends over to the house. Momma told her she didn't want her friends coming over anymore. My sister got mad asking momma why. Momma shouted back with annoyance, thinking she knew better to ask her such a question. My sister knew momma

Joy M. Pierre

made all the rules but didn't care what came out of her mouth at times. She disrespectfully told momma that she didn't have to listen to her rules. Why did she say that? Momma's face frowned and she bit the bottom of her lip jogging over, reaching toward her face with one hand. My sister was lifted up by her neck and threw into the wall with her feet dangling, grasping for air. She tried to loosen momma's grip, but it kept getting tighter. Momma wasn't letting go. I felt paralyzed. I couldn't believe what I was witnessing. Not able to move I kept yelling at momma telling her to let go. But it was as if momma had zoned-out. She wasn't paying attention to me, blocking out the noises. Luckily, my brother came home and caught momma in action. He jumped in to help my sister. Momma wrestled my brother with one hand while she still had sister threw against the wall with the other.

Momma looked her in the eyes telling her she would kill her. But my sister couldn't say anything back. All I heard was a choking sound. Momma was still trying to throw my brother off of her. But she had a grip of death on him too. My brother managed to loosen the grip on my sister's neck. Momma let go. My sister fell to the ground coughing and choking more. Momma turned toward my brother like as if looks could kill, running in his direction. He was fast, momma would have never caught him, but she kept trying.

I looked up again, and he was running, and my sister was too. And I was trying to get out of the way so I didn't get ran over. Everyone stopped running, breathing hard. My sister shot behind my brother for protection. Momma was cursing the both of them out for attacking her. I could clearly see my sister was seconds away from death and momma was telling them that she wasn't going to kill her, and they shouldn't have double team her.

They left out the front door backwards, keeping their eyes on momma. I was still there with her and I thought she was going to do something to me because she couldn't get to them. Momma didn't look my way, and I was panicking. She left the room, and I sat down thinking about what just happened. If it wasn't for my brother, I believe momma would have choked her to death. I felt her anger came from her childhood experiences. But she never told me any stories of her parents doing that to her. I felt that my parents were good role models until I saw momma choking my sister. I knew she had her reasons for what she did, but that didn't give her the privilege to try and kill her own daughter. Momma loved us all dearly; so I thought. When I saw what she did, I began to look at things differently. It never failed, momma was always after her.

Another day my sister made her mad. It was over the same stuff. Momma thought that she was trying to hook her friends up with my dad. They were arguing back and forth. They stood at the top of our upstairs in the hallway. Momma threw her against the wall again. I wished my brother was home, but it was our other sister and I. My other sister kept yelling, telling momma to leave her alone, but momma wasn't listening. We always felt it was the right thing to say, but it was just a waste of breath. I walked up to momma and grabbed her free arm that time. Why did I do that? Momma threw me into the wall. I hit my head and my back hard, falling onto the floor. My eyes bulged. I couldn't believe how momma was treating us. I started screaming as if I was in terrible pain. Momma let her loose and turned around to look at me, seeing if I was okay. I was okay but anything was worth a try when she attacked us. Momma's grip was so tight around her neck that she was gasping for air. Both of my sisters ran down the steps out of the house. I got off the floor and took off past momma running after them.

They were walking toward the Video Store at the corner of Frost Street and Third Avenue. I was waving my hands running behind them to catch up, but they kept walking. I made it to the edge of the store and they snatched my shirt pulling me. They knew something that I didn't know. We peeked around the corner and momma was following us. She was walking toward our direction with a steel baseball bat in her hand. I was scared and my sisters were coming up with a plan. I knew she was going to kill us. The closer she came toward us we panicked and paced the pavement. We couldn't walk over our friend's house because we knew she wouldn't hesitate going there. We looked again and momma had turned around walking back to the house. We all walked over to our friend's house thinking how mean and crazy she was for coming after us. They both decided that it was best if I went back home, but told me they were running away. I told them I was running away too. But they told me I was too young to run away, and that I needed to go back home. I walked off, not looking forward to seeing the look on momma's face when she saw I was back. All I could think was, what if it was a set-up and she hurt me, who would save me? I kept walking because I had no other place to go, plus I was hungry. I was mad at them for making me go back. After seeing that bat in momma's hand; why would anybody want to go back? I went home, and momma was sitting on the couch smoking a cigarette like she was waiting on me. I walked on the other side of the room and she spoke. I jumped. She asked me where my crazy sisters were, and I told her they ran away, and I didn't know where they went. All she said was that they would be back, as she shook her head. My sisters didn't come back home for a long time, but, I knew where they were. We all had the same friends. When they stayed away for a while momma missed them and was happy to see them. She acted like she was never mad.

I also remember the days my dad went roller skating. I never saw any emotions on momma's face the nights he would leave. With no respect, he left the house late at nights and returned early mornings. He had his own routines. He went to work, came home to the garage, went into the house to use the bathroom, got some food, took it back to the garage and ate. Then went back into the house and shaved, washed up, put on his clothes, spray on a lot of colognes, and leave going skating. Something changed. She did something strange, that made me feel that she didn't trust my dad, and could have possibly felt he was cheating on her. So she got tired of his routines.

One day, Momma was being spontaneous. Our neighbors were an older married couple, who ran a small business out of their home. The wife rode around in an electric wheelchair when she wasn't in the house. Not to mention they had vicious dogs that were angry whenever we pulled into the driveway or walked in and out of our house. One day, the neighbor came over to the house asking to speak to my dad. But he wasn't there. Momma was upstairs, so we didn't bother her. He never came over before so we all were curious why he'd knock at our door. He came back over to our house when his dogs alarmed him that my dad was pulling in the driveway.

There were a few knocks at the door and momma ran to open it smiling. She hoped he was there for her, but he asked to speak with my dad. Momma went to get him and they all stood at the front door chatting. My dad walked away from the door disappointed. And momma stood there with a blank expression on her face. My dad yelled asking momma why she wrote the letter. But mom-

70   Joy M. Pierre

ma denied it all. They went back and forth arguing for a while. We were clueless about what happened. The more we listened to them, the more information we found out. Momma had written a love letter to the neighbor. The letter was about how she wanted to sex him up. But what was strange was, she got past those vicious dogs putting it under the windshield blades of his truck in his gated backyard. My sisters, brother, and I laughed.

We bypass the part about her writing the letter and focused on how she got over the fence to his car, and put it under the windshield wipers without their dogs catching her. We asked her how she did it, but all she did was smile and laugh. She thought it was funny. I thought maybe they put the dogs up at a certain time and since she didn't have a job; she learned their routines. He was a married man and momma didn't care that his wife was there. As sad as it was, she never told us how it happened.

One rainy day I sat on the couch, tilting a flute glass to my mouth. Hard drops hit the window blurring my vision. Loud tires were squealing from the rude neighbors. I jumped up to look outside to see the drama. It was a shame what I saw. It was a couple of young guys showing off in classic cars. The cars reminded me of a car I saw a long time ago at my high school. I sat on the parking lot curb waiting for my sister when a 1985 burgundy and maroon two-toned Monte Carlo pulled up in front of me. One guy jumped out the car stumbling in my direction. I couldn't see the driver's face because his seat was leaned back as far as it could go. But he was peeking out the window watching everything. I stood up, defenseless, and outnumbered. The one in front of me reached down in the front of his pants drawing his hand back. Out of fear, my eyes bulged. I thought I was tough but my heart kept racing and was about to jump out my chest. I didn't know what to expect. He stared me in the eyes with hatred coming closer and closer. I back away when I saw him holding a black shiny object. I didn't know what it was, but I knew what I didn't want it to be. I panicked forgetting to breathe, wishing it all was a dream. His lips were moving, but no words came out. By then he knew he had full control over my life. He saw my shoulders rise and my shaky hands. The only thing that mattered, was what he was holding. As he came closer I realized it was a gun. My body froze. He pushed the hard metal into my stomach, making my body jump. Knowing I only had seconds to live I begged for my life.

In an angry voice, he forced me to give him money patting my pockets. I didn't have any to give him. He yelled a second time, demanding money. I reached into my pocket gripping the money with a fist. I swung my hand out and shoved it to him. He snatched it, stuffing his pocket. I back up to walk away and he shook the gun at me telling me not to move. He looked me up and down demanding my rings which were the only things I had to remind me of momma. I hated to give them up, but he left me no choice. I grabbed my instrument and tried to walk off again but he ordered me to hand it over. He snatched it taking it back to the car. It traumatized me. I never expected something like that to happen. I watched him run back over to me. That's when I knew I would hear a gunshot. He pointed it to my face and told me not to tell. I turned my eyes in the opposite direction telling him okay. He ran the barrel of the gun down my shirt to the last button. In a soft tone, he told me to take off my shirt. By then, I was fed up and told him no begging him not to take my shirt too. The driver shouted telling him lets go. He threatened me one last time and ran back, jumped into the car, and slammed the door laughing, and high fiving the driver. The driver slammed on the gas pedal.

Joy M. Pierre

The car didn't move. But white clouds of smoke and the smell of burnt rubber filled the air. The car peeled off and vanished.

As bad as I wanted to defend myself, my life could have been easily taken. We all say what we would do if that ever happened, but in reality, none of us knows if we'll run, scream, fight back, stare the eye of the opponent or get shot. No one asks to be violated or disrespected. From time to time I took life for granted or was at the wrong place at the wrong time. Make sure it's not you. Guard your footprints, life happens at the end of your comfort zone.

Chapter 5

With attempts to promote a happy, and balanced life, I failed. I took a leap of faith to see how far I would come. But the ordinary part of life still wasn't good enough. Yeah, I thought I closed chapters, but I didn't. They were wide open. No one could tell me I wasn't normal but when life gave me difficulties, I had no manual with instructions. The reality of pain, trust, neglect, and tears affected my visions on how I saw things. But my only choice was to do as I was taught and I wasn't. I locked myself in the car, making sure no one could get in. My reclined seat made me stare up looking at the ceiling. I closed my eyes reaching for the volume knob to the radio. It was one of my favorite songs playing. So I turned up the volume. I thought back to the time I was feeling that same way. After momma died, my dad put up some books of hers that said magic on the front cover. He was out of his room on his routine visits to the garage. I snuck into the room tip-toeing and peeking through drawers. I knew they had to have been there, so I kept looking. I ran to the closet with hopes of not getting caught. I peeked my head in and saw the shotgun leaned against the wall. Out of curiosity, I touched the hard metal on the barrel. I shook my head and snatched my hand back to focus on finding the books. I reached for the pile of clothes lifting them. I smiled and was relieved. I had found them. I snatched the books and rushed back to my room, closing and locking my door.

I opened the book and begun to read, but they were weird. None of the words made sense. I kept reading and reading until I became frustrated. The books weren't helping. I wanted to know why momma committed suicide. I wondered was it the books, my dad, or us kids that pushed her to the limits.

A few days later, I pulled those same books out flipping through the pages. I mentally felt alone. I sat on my bed thinking. The room was quiet. I looked up at my wall of a family photo that we took, when I was in the fifth grade. The longer I stared the more memories I formed. I looked at momma in the picture as tears rolled down my face. I fell, and broke down to my knees on the bedroom floor. The next moment I was punching the floor. I was missing momma badly and wanted to be with her again. I had a model airplane made of steel. It was somewhat heavy. I picked it up wishing I could fly away. But I was stuck living with my dad who treated me like I didn't exist. I lifted the airplane and smacked it against my head. The more I did it, the more force was used. I kept doing it hoping to knock myself out. I jumped from the floor running placing my back against the door. I was still breathing. I could still see everything the same. I could still function. But only to have a major headache still wasn't good enough.

Joy M. Pierre

I yanked the door handle, and swung it open hitting the wall. I was in a rage. I came out of my bedroom holding the metal object as a weapon. I wiped my tears walking toward my dad's room yelling his name. Usually, he wouldn't have been there but he was at that time. I stood in his doorway when he looked up at me sitting in a chair. I told him he was the reason my momma died and called him a killer. He jumped up, and I kept yelling I wanted momma back, and I'm going to find her. When I saw how fast he jumped, I ran to the stairwell running down half the steps and jumping the rest running into the wall. I caught my balance and ran out the front door. He was behind me hoping not to see or hear a repeat of momma.

He tried to calm me down telling me to come back inside. I yelled causing confusion for the neighbors telling him he killed momma. Not caring if I hurt his feeling, I kept repeating it until he blurted it wasn't his fault. I told him he was still responsible for her death; he could have stopped her. He stepped into the porch with one foot propping the door open, telling me he was taking me to the hospital. I had a bruise on my forehead that was bleeding. I looked down in my hand, I never let the metal object go so I dropped it on the ground and walked toward the porch sitting on the steps. I was exhausted.

He took me to one of the scariest parts of the hospital. Hurley Hospital had a unit for kids that were acting like me. The doctor asked me what happened and I was honest. I told him I missed momma. The doctor told me I had to stay there for a couple of days for observation to make sure everything was okay. I didn't want to go back home with my dad so I agreed. A couple of nurses took me to an elevator with special access. I looked up at my dad because I was getting nervous. He looked back at me and gave me a fake smile. I started panicking. The elevator door opened. I hid behind him holding onto the back of his shirt.

He kept walking and I was pulling him back so we could leave. I was on the crazy floor. I heard loud noises of yelling, screaming, and fist pounding on the walls. I jumped looking side to side. Those same lovely nurses I met with the doctor were the total opposite when we got off the elevator. One nurse told me to calm down or she would give me something to calm me. I looked at her with an evil eye. I wasn't crazy, but she was. I was just missing momma. A girl ran past me bumping my shoulder. I turned to look at her, but before I could turn back around a powerful wind passed me, startling me. I made it to the room surprisingly.

I wanted to go home. My room at home was better than that one. I thought going there was a good thing. I was fooled. I sat on a worn hard bed that creaked. I could tell it was old because you could feel the circles from the springs popping out. I was told to put all my personal belongings in a zip-lock bag. The nurse took my jewelry, belts, shoe strings, and hair ties. She said I wouldn't need them until I left. I felt like she robbed me. My dad was looking and said nothing. We all left the room and walked to a community room. I heard a girl screaming. That gush of powerful wind that rushed by me earlier were those nurses with a needle running after her to sedate her. I took a deep breath and looked at my dad he was jiggling his keys. I looked him in the eyes and told him not to leave me. He gave me a quick hug and walked off. He was walking away and I was calling his name telling him not to leave me, but he kept going. I was mad. Momma would have never done that. I felt that he had thrown me away. When momma died, it felt as if a part of me left too. Maybe I looked like momma and he couldn't stand it. It always felt as if he had something against me.

I sat at a table with my hand on the side of my face, looking around. It was a lot going on, to focus on one person. I heard someone calling my name. I turned around and saw it was that same nurse again. She was talking to me in a sweet voice.

I gave her a fake smirk and turned back facing forward. She called my name again and I sighed, standing up. I looked at her and saw her hand jester to come her way. I walked toward her in slow motion stopping in my tracks. A ball flew past my face. I looked in the direction it came from, a girl stood feet away laughing. I kept walking knowing I would have gotten a tranquilizer shot if I took a detour. She handed me a small clear cup with a pink pill inside. I never saw a pill like that and she was anxious for me to take it. I didn't know what it would do, so I asked. She told me the pill would make me feel better and calm me down. I knew it was all a lie and she was trying to get her way. If you asked me, I was calmer than she was. It was her joker face smile that frightened me. So I reached my hand out and grabbed the pill cup, looking inside. I looked up, and she was standing hovering over me watching. I had no choice but to lean back, shaking the pill in my mouth. She gave me a cup of water and I tried to walk away. She stopped me and told me to take it. I looked back at her again and took a sip of water pretended to swallow it, walking away. She told me to stop while she walked toward me. She put on her latex gloves popping them against her wrist. She frowned and told me to open my mouth.

I took her as a joke and opened my mouth. There was no pill. Then she told me to lift my tongue as she reached into my mouth with her fingers. She caught me. She gave me more water so I could swallow the pill. We stood there until I swallowed it. But that was the first time I remembered taking pills, so it wasn't easy.

A few minutes later, I felt strange. I never felt like that before. I sat down, feeling like the world was spinning. I tried to get back up, but it was hard. It felt like a ton of weights was pressing me down. I wanted to rest, but the only time we were allowed in our room was at bedtime. They kept us all in the same area so they could monitor us all together. By the time the pill wore off I was mentally exhausted by bedtime. I had many crying and restless nights. I knew I had to get out of there one day, and I wasn't going back. The lonely feeling made me more depressed. All I wanted was to get out of there and for my dad to show me love. Every day was the same routine, eat, medication, sit around, medication, and sleep. Two weeks went by slow. I knew it was time for me to leave, but I was a different person. I felt worse than before. I couldn't function because the medication pacified my true personality. I was just existing, but I wasn't living. I hated myself and everyone else too.

My dad walked through the door to pick me up. I was happy that he hadn't forgotten about me. I made it home. I ran to my room and someone had changed it around. Something was missing. The family photo was gone from my wall. I asked my dad about it. He told he put it up so I wouldn't reminisce about it. At the time, I felt he should have left it where it was. I didn't understand why he took something from me knowing it would make me mad. I thought a better approach would have been for him to sit down with me to discuss my problems. I felt he should have made a greater effort, both physically and emotionally. He never hugged or told me he loved me.

Joy M. Pierre

I opened my eyes. I hated when my mind drifted back to the past. But the feelings from the past never left. I hated myself back then and I hated myself at that moment. Tears welled my eyes and dribbled down my cheeks. That wasn't the cry of grief but the cry of hatred. I pulled a small brown bottle out the console of the car throwing it to the passenger seat. I reached in the back seat and grabbed a water bottle. I turned the volume of the radio louder to drown out the feelings I was experiencing. I thought getting my mind more involved with the music would help me with my decisions. It made it worse. With the bottled water in one hand, I reached for the steering wheel with the other to rise up. I placed my head in the center of the steering wheel even overwhelmed by why I was in that situation. My mind was all over the place. I took a deep breath and grabbed the pill bottle too, looking at them both. I tried to open it but that doggone child safety lock had jammed. I felt it was a sign to stop. But the feeling of hate was greater. I rose my seat to support my back and I tried to open it again. It popped open. Before I had a second thought I shoved them in my mouth and drank the water. I was choking and gagging. I swallowed some and some were spit out. I sat there for a while waiting for it to happen.

I waited for my world to end. I felt dizzy and fatigue looking down from the pressure. I heard a loud tap on the window and it startled me. I looked up at the window my vision was blurry. I must have moved too fast because my head was throbbing and I was dizzier. I squinted my eyes trying to focus on who it was on the other side of the window. I kept hearing a faint voice. I kept shaking my head to overcome the feeling that came over me but I couldn't. I was too late. There was no way of calming it down, and the tapping was getting louder and louder.

My body felt numb, I tried to reach for the door handle, but couldn't move my arms or legs. I had forgotten that I was locked in the car. The more banging I heard focused my attention on the noise. I grabbed the door handle with force jiggling it to break out as if they were the one that needed rescuing. I forgot to unlock it. After many attempts, my mind registered that I needed to unlock the door. I reached for it and yanked it open. The door swung open and it was my closest friend. She saw the pills spilled all over. She panicked because she didn't know how long I was there, telling me I messed up the churches money meaning I had no business doing what I did. She threatened to call 911. I begged her not to. I was embarrassed that she caught me, and I didn't want anyone else to know what I did. I knew others would think I was crazy, but I wasn't. I was tired of feeling alone. I was tired of trying to figure out life. I was tired of being neglected. I was tired of making excuses for my dad, and I was tired of reliving that gunshot moment from momma.

My friend knew me well because I introduced her to my life, knowing she had a choice to accept me or not. Even though she didn't call 911 she drove me to McLaren hospital keeping me alert. She knew if I didn't fall asleep, I would be okay. I could hear her talking but couldn't make sense of what she was saying. She sounded like a broken record player that was bothering my nerves. She did right by taking me to the hospital. The first time I was just missing momma but that time I really wanted to be with momma.

At the hospital, I had two choices I could either drink a charcoal mixture or have a tube put down my throat to flush my stomach. I chose the awful charcoal I had to finish before I saw the doctor. They advised me to stay for observation. As bad as I didn't want to stay I knew my friend wouldn't take me back home. I was mad at her, and I felt as if she was throwing me away too. Two nurses took me to my room on the seventh floor. It was nothing like when I was at Hurley Hospital. The floor was full of youngsters, but McLaren had older folks. I knew people had mental health issues, and knew not to judge them, but at McLaren people did things I didn't, like talking to themselves, saw ghosts, cut themselves, and did harsh things to other people. I knew I wasn't insane, but I felt I would have been before I left. I was in a cry for help, not segregation.

I met a girl who was the same age as me that dealt with similar situations. She smoked cigarettes just like I did, so I freeloaded on her. She got discharged before me, and went home to deal with the real world again. We stayed in touch. We promised each other to deal with our past more seriously and to get through our future encounters.

The more we talked the closer our friendship formed. I called her days after I got out of the hospital, her mom answered. All the times we spoke her mom never answered so I knew something was strange. I went to sit down when I heard the pain in her mom's voice. She told me that my friend jumped from a school building. I asked her if she was dead before she could finish talking. She told me that she was caught and was back inside the hospital. She couldn't function without the hospital and it became her home. I was hurt. I couldn't call the hospital. They only allowed visitations and I had no way to speak with her to be put on the list. We lost touch with each other, and I never spoke of her again.

I wasn't any better than my friend. After those two long weeks of discipline, I felt love and attention from the staff. I wasn't an afterthought. I didn't realize, but I was most definitely around others dealing with similar situations, but I judged their appearance. As for the medication that made me a zombie, I wasn't going back. I knew when I got out I had to face life and deal with my issues. I was happy to be home but sad to know that all the problems were still there. But when I thought about my friend I told myself if things ever got bad again I'd have a place to go that would save my life. My dad promised me counseling, but there was no effort or support to make it happen. Those treatment days in the hospitals were the only counseling I received. My journey wasn't easy, but I learned a long time ago to care for myself. I had to mature at a young age. His busyness forced me to be responsible. I didn't have a childhood, and I was emotionally abused. Everything seemed good on the outside, but on the inside, I was screaming like Hell on earth. I didn't realize I apologized for others behaviors when they did something wrong to build them.

I over thought everything people said or done because I wanted to prepare for the worst. I downplayed many of my problems convincing myself they weren't that bad, so I could avoid them. I felt like I was a liability. I bottled everything up, not wanting help for myself. I used to tell people yes when I really meant no. I use to lose confidence when people raised their voice at me. I use to be silent and not speak up for myself because I thought it would cause more pain. I use to feel like I was stupid and could never trust myself because others didn't trust me. I knew I was gullible. I would believe anything someone told me. I would do whatever someone told me to do, with no questions asked. I always wanted my life to run smoothly, but being passive didn't make my life easier. And I shaped all that from momma and living without her. I thought when momma left, the responsibility was

Joy M. Pierre

passed on to my dad. I just wanted him to love me and be kind. I wanted him to tell me that he loved me so I could have the motivation to conquer things in life with support. I wished he was a person that listened, telling me everything would have been okay. I wished when things were wrong, he showed patience for me. I wanted him to be strong and take ownership that he had children. He never told me he was proud of me and I wish he had. I wished I knew him mentally.

Pain for me was more natural than breathing. I had experienced a lot. That void couldn't be filled with material things. The pain I felt was normal, it was an addiction my life needed, to get by. The first time I felt that pain was the day momma passed away. I felt throbbing. My mind was racing ten thousand miles per hour. My heart was beating so fast that, the second I felt it, I thought it was going to run away from my body, and it was shattered. My smiles instantly turned to frowns, complete with tears. My body weakened and went limp. I was in shock. I rested on my knees hoping my heart would stop racing. The pain had taken over me completely. I was wishing my body to go into full overdrive, but it didn't. I wanted to get up and ask all the questions I could get an answer for, but everyone looked like a ghost. Even though I never ask for the pain, I received it anyway. My heart was painful, and there was no one to save me.

I never recovered from it, I suppress it at times. A lot of things that I experienced through life had invaded my mind, leaving a gigantic opening for other dreadful things to enter into it. I was the only person who could have eliminated the pain that had taken over me. At the time I wanted to eliminate it, but I had a change of heart, it was attached to momma. From that pain, I gained knowledge about taking things for granted. I use to wonder how others dealt with the pain of losing a loved one. I was told before, just forget about it and let the dead be dead. That was easier said than done. I didn't forget. As my life went on, it didn't get any easier to deal with the passion. I had chest pain from a broken heart. There was no place to run or hide. No one understood what I was going through because they never experienced the storms I had. But I knew when they lost a loved one they would understand that pain was like a sickness.

But I had experienced more. Thinking back to the time when I was pregnant with my son. It was another hot, summer day at 7-Eleven as my co-worker and I put some old, stale hot dogs into a box for my dog. I was looking forward to a calm, relaxed evening in my backyard without any distractions. All I really wanted to hear were birds chirping, instead of my noisy neighbor's dogs barking. She loved hot dogs; I knew my neighbor's dogs would probably love them too. That day was the day I put it to the test.

I made it home, and my brown-and-white undersized pit bull ran toward me. She was anxious, jumping up to get my box of wieners. I gave her one, and she begged for more. Usually, I dumped the leftovers, but that time I wanted to shut those dogs up and test the effectiveness of the magical steaming hot dogs. I took three hot dogs out of the box, smiling because I knew I would get their attention. Confidently, I walked down my steps, out the back door, and into my backyard toward the fence. The dogs hesitantly approached the fence, staring at me as if I were the captain of an army platoon. Suddenly, the unsure hounds began to bark with ferocity. Only their owner would have been able to calm them down. I daringly dangled a piece of a hot dog over the fence and tossed it within the dogs reach. The first dog chomped four times,

Joy M. Pierre

and the hot dog was gone. He ate it so fast it slipped down his throat. I threw the other hot dog farther, hoping the female dog would get the meat. She scavenged around for it, found it, and chomped until all the hot dog was in her mouth. She gnawed the hot dog three times, and it disappeared down her throat.

I wondered if the dogs were really hungry or was the food extremely good. They happily ate the hot dogs. A third dog was kept chained to the fence because he was aggressive. He salivated, waiting for a piece, but he was too far from my reach, to throw it that far. I broke the third hot dog in half to give the two unchained dog's one last taste of the stale hot dogs. I knew the dogs wouldn't mind having another portion because of how greedily they ate the first one. They gobbled their halves quickly as if they were swallowing some kind of secret. They were completely silent, licking their chops and staring at me. I gave them something that tasted so delicious. I felt the hot dogs were working. I had a chance of them liking me. Them liking me would have helped me enjoy my backyard. I looked into their eyes, stunned. They continued licking every remnant of the hot dogs from around their mouths and snouts. Their eyes were begging me to give them more.

The male was standing at full salute toward the fence, and the female was about five feet behind him. I took another hot dog from the box, broke it in half, and tossed one piece to the male dog. Then I threw the second piece further for the female. In a blink of an eye, the male dog had finished his portion and raced toward her share. She snarled and growled. The hair on the back of her neck stood erect and her tail stuck out like a sore thumb. The male's lips begin to tremble as he bared his fangs in an attempt to persuade his adversary to back down. They both began growling, eye to eye, circling each other. They had teeth like vampires, and they were salivating, the saliva ran down their teeth, dripping into the grass, and drip after drip. I shouted telling them to stop. But there was no way I was going to jump that four-foot raggedy fence and get between them. They charged toward each other as a bull charges a matador in a bullfight. My mouth dropped. I watched them battle for a whole minute. I knew I did something wrong. They were fighting, and you could see hatred in their demon eyes as they shook each other's body from side to side with their mouth.

They gave each other bear hugs and tore large clots of fur from each other's body. The rest of their fur was bloody, from ripping each other's flesh. Blood was spurting on the grass like it was coming from a water hose. It looked like the dogs had mowed the lawn with it because I saw it everywhere. They knocked over a large dog house and several garbage cans. The backyard was in complete chaos. In the course of the fight, the male dog pinned the female on her back several times, shaking her by the neck. She managed to hold him off long enough to exhaust him, while she struggled to get up. Even though she wasn't as quick as him, she kept fighting. She knew a load of puppies were in her belly. She knew it was only going to be one winner, so she continued fighting, locking her bloody jaws into him. It was frightening.

I knew my blood pressure had increased as I swiftly walked, barefoot back into the house. I didn't know what to do so I raised my hands to the Lord, panicking and pacing the floor. My body got weak. I rushed around the corner to my neighbor's front door, gasping for air. I banged on the door until someone opened it. My neighbor snatched the door open, and I shouted that his dogs were fighting, all in one breath. The neighbor said nothing, running to his backyard to see if I was being truthful. I heard him yelling so I went back home. I could still hear the commotion. He was using a lot of profanity, not to mention the dogs were still fighting. I hesitated to look at them because I had seen enough. They were killing themselves.

I made it back home and ran into the house sitting my overwhelmed body on the couch, sighing. I felt terrible. An hour later I went back outside to see if his dogs were okay. He was standing in the backyard cleaning up trash that fell out the waste can from the brawl. I didn't mention to him about those stale hot dogs. I was paranoid he would find that piece that I threw over the fence. He did look up and thanked me for informing him his dogs were at war. I saw the disappointment on his face but he was calm as if the situation happened before. The stud killed the female dog and her ten puppies. I sadly went back into the house, shaking my head. I couldn't believe what I saw and heard. I was an unintentional murderer. My intent had been to win the dogs over with the stale hot dogs. I never told that neighbor that I gave the dog's one last taste. I knew he would have killed my dog. He didn't appear to be a crazy guy, but I knew he would have taken revenge for the pain I caused. I knew better to attempt that situation again and mind my own business. I lived with that guilt and it caused me a lot of heartache and pain. I was a dog lover.

Chapter 6

I remembered a former Flint councilman of the Fifth Ward in Flint, Michigan. Fred Tucker was known as a master of political footwork. He was successful because he understood human nature and took advantage of people's weaknesses and prejudices. He came to Flint in 1949 from Albion and worked at Buick from 1950 to 1965. He was a union official at UAW Local 599 and a member of the NAACP and the Urban League of Flint. He later left Buick to run his own business in realty and insurance. In 1952 he got married and had five daughters. His relationship with his wife was stormy. One day she showed up at the City Hall with a gun, demanding to see him. Tucker then went to Las Vegas for a while to lie low until things calmed down between them. He took time out to work on their differences, and in hopes of repairing his marriage. Another time at a council's committee meeting, Tucker and his wife's voice raised at one another. The entire council turns in their direction to make sense of what the fuss was about. Not realizing they became the focus in the council's committee room. He was forced to quiet her down in front of everyone. But the arguing continued. No one really knew the reasoning behind the arguments, but they knew they weren't professional.

In 1970, Tucker and Flint's mayor was indicted by a grand jury. They were convicted of gambling and accepting bribes for favorable votes on a public-housing project. Despite these convictions, Tucker still won re-election by 56 votes. In 1976, Tucker was appointed an administrator of the struggling Flint General Hospital.

He was then charged with using hospital employees and material to make repairs on some houses he owned and was also accused of other wrongdoings. In the late 70s, Tucker divorced his wife and found himself a new bride. In 1980, Tucker and his bride were married in Toledo, Ohio. The weddings plans were made well before he learned the death of his ex-wife. But he went to her wake in Lansing, Michigan. That was the last time anyone saw Tucker and his new wife alive.

Tucker and his new bride of five days disappeared. Friends became concerned when Tucker did not appear at his ex-wife's funeral. They said that he made all the arrangements and had offered to give the eulogy. They went to Tucker's Flint home and saw that there had been a forced entry.

The police feared foul play when they found his wallet with a driver license and no money. They also said pillowcases and sheets were missing. Pieces of rope were scattered around the property. The whole house had been ransacked. Steak knives were scattered all over the kitchen table. It appeared that someone had carelessly cleaned the kitchen floor. His wife's car was in the driveway, but Tucker's car was missing. The detectives felt that the burglar had taken advantage of the ex-wife's funeral to break into his house. Tucker could have surprised the intruders, and him and his wife could have been abducted. Maybe he could have been in financial trouble because of another business he owned. If that was true, Tucker still had no reason to borrow money from the loan sharks, because he had money.

The police continued searching for Tucker and his wife. They found his car in a parking lot of a south-side bar on Atherton Road. A resident of the city read an article about his car missing and called it into the police. The car fit the description of Tucker's 1979 Buick Riviera. The car was covered in snow, which made the police believe that it had been parked there for a couple of days. The car was unlocked, and the keys were missing. In the front seat was a pepper-like substance, similar to the substance found on the kitchen floor of Tucker's home.

The detectives were still hoping to find them alive because they didn't want to assume that Tucker and his wife were dead. But there was a great chance that they had been abducted. In the trunk of Tucker's car were strands of rope similar to the strands that were found on his kitchen floor.

Tucker and his bride were exterminated. They were suffocated, and their bodies were found in a Toledo, Ohio, dump. Over one-hundred miles away from Flint. The police believed at least two men abducted them.

Authorities and family guessed that the murders could have been caused by hit men. He could have been in some trouble with political enemies or one of his businesses. Some way someone knew his routine and caught him off guard. He was a person with a lot of power and influence to the community that carried a gun in his waistband.

Fred Tucker was a United Automobile Workers committeeman for Buick. He was also involved in real estate, construction, and insurance, a member of the NAACP and the Urban League of Flint, and management of Flint General Hospital. With all of the accomplishments under his belt, he was only 49 years old when he was murdered.

To this day, his murder is still an unsolved mystery. That story touched my heart. I wasn't related to Tucker, but his impressionable visions for the city stood out. I believe, Flint lost a great asset. He was involved in every aspect of the community, to make a better city.

There are many more people who didn't get a chance to make an impact on the community because their life was taken. Here are a few murders that remained unsolved.

A twenty-one-year-old walked into a tavern on Industrial Avenue. She asked if someone could call an ambulance, then she collapsed. Later, they saw blood soaking through her thick winter coat, finding she had been stabbed repeatedly.

Someone shot a twenty-seven-year-old while standing on Winona Street by a drive-by. His wife heard dogs barking. She glanced out the window to see why and saw a man lying on the ground. It was her husband.

Someone shot a forty-three-year-old several times at Wand-A-Magic Car Wash on North Saginaw. He was only passing through to wash his truck after a hard day of work.

A fifty-six-year-old man was found dead in his car on Root Street. Someone shot him in the head during a robbery.

Someone shot a thirty-two-year-old several times at his house on McClellan Street. The house was set on fire with the intent to cover the crime.

Someone shot a thirty-three-year-old in the head at a friend's house on Dupont Street, during a rainstorm.

Someone shot a thirty-two-year-old man to death on Baltimore Street by a female acquaintance who had stopped by for a casual visit.

Someone shot a forty-year-old woman in the kitchen of her apartment on East Twelfth Street.

I imagined all the stories that never made it to the mass media. Many of them went unnoticed. This is another story I felt passionate about that never made headlines.

I had a cousin I perceived as sweet, but others knew her as more than outspoken. I didn't know if her behavior trickled from something else or because she grew up without her biological parents. At a young age, her dad was shot to death. And her mom was serving a life sentenced in prison for killing him. She lived with her granny in another city an hour away. When she came to Flint, it was only for short visits. One time she came, my cousin and her friend walked to Dion's Mini-Mart on the west side of Flint. Back then, it was cool to get out and walk, even if you had a car. It was the way we mingled and connected with our friends since we had no social media like Facebook, Twitter, or Instagram to follow them on. Making it to the store, they pushed the door open hearing a loud chime that alarmed clerks of their entrance. They already knew what they wanted, so they grabbed a pop, and a beer and headed to the counter. We had Bottle men that stood close to an empty grocery basket that counted recycled bottles. They were also in charge of restocking the coolers and watched over the store for thieves. He approached my cousin with a conversation while she was asking for cigarettes.

Her friend saw her neighbor. She walked over to him making a casual conversation. They lived on the same street so she asked him for a ride back home. Back then neighbors looked out for each other. All three of them left the store and got in his car. But my cousin realized she didn't have her cigarettes, so she jumped out and ran back into the store, while they waited. Her friend and her neighbor continued to small talk, then she realized my cousin was taking too long to come out of the store. She jumped out of the car and slammed the door running back in to get her. The door swung open and my cousin turned to look at her. She was shocked to see my cousin's face swollen and marked up within only minutes. It looked like she had gotten into a fight. Money was on the floor behind her. Apparently, my cousin had a way of using her words that offended others. Her friend grabbed her and said it was time to go before things got more out of hand. My cousin asked if she could pick up her money from the floor. Without hesitation, she reached down to grab it. Before she could grab the money, a gun was pointed to her head.

The Bottleman told her to leave the money and get up. My cousin tried to rush over to her but was stopped by a hug from him telling her everything was alright. She turned loose and grabbed her friend, to leave the store.

Joy M. Pierre

They thought they were walking away from him, but he was a couple of steps behind them heading out of the store too. He asked my cousin if she knew him; she told him no. Then he responded by telling them that wasn't good enough, and how they were about to die.

He fired a shot in the air and then shot my cousin in the head. Her friend watched her hit the ground while she charged toward him wrestling for the gun. As they tussled, he shot her in the head too, but she was still conscious. She laid on the ground playing dead waiting for him to leave. He went back into the store with the gun in his hand telling the clerk they didn't have to worry about them anymore. She came from behind the counter walking toward the door to look outside. She saw two bodies on the ground. She grabbed her mouth in shock, hoping she wasn't next. He asked if she was going to tell on him, and she said no walking away from the door. She told him that she didn't see anything.

While he was in the store with the clerk, my cousin's friend got up checking on my cousin's pulse to see if she was alive. My cousin was unresponsive, so she ran down the street to a friend's house for help. He went back outside, and the clerk ran toward the door shaking. She grabbed the door handle and pulled it toward her, locking it. She called 911, the store owner, and her parents to tell what she had witnessed. She turned off the lights and waited in the cooler until the police came. The Bottleman was standing outside the door of the store when the police arrived. He was pretended to be talking to someone inside. They questioned him, he told them he only saw three black males running by when he heard the gunshots.

They didn't notice blood on his face, hands, or upper

body, and there was no gun. The officers put him in the patrol car and tried to get the clerk to open the store, but she was too hysterical to unlock the door.

With their backs turned the Bottleman climb to the front seat of the patrol car, forcing the door open with his shoulder, and took off. The officers chased and arrested him. A few minutes later, a man told an officer that he saw the Bottleman take a gun to a house a block away and gave it to two black males. He gave information but didn't want to get involved and refused to give his name.

The police rushed to the address, to follow up on the lead. They identified themselves while banging on the door. With no search warrant, the owner didn't open. Finally, someone opened after 40 minutes. A .357 magnum was found in a paper bag in an air duct of the hallway floor.

Back at the store, the police calmed the frantic clerk to get a statement. She told the police before the shooting, the Bottleman showed her he had a gun in his pocket. My cousin and her friend went into the store around 1 a.m. and conversed with the Bottleman. They left the store, but cousin came back in for cigarettes. She rang up the purchase, and my cousin paid with a twenty-dollar bill. She gave her back seventeen dollars in change, all in singles. While my cousin was counting her change, the Bottleman blurted out, asking if she called him out his name. She didn't respond but kept counting her change.

He walked up to my cousin grabbing her head banging it against the counter repeatedly. It swelled my cousin's face when he finally stopped. The clerk told her to leave the store. She placed a call to another store asking for help. She stated she didn't know exactly what he did next, while she was on the phone. All she claimed to see

Joy M. Pierre

was my cousin and the Bottleman leave the store. Minutes later she heard three gunshots, and dropped to the floor because they were close.

After the trial, he was found guilty of first-degree murder, assault with intent to commit murder, and with a felony firearm. And was sentenced to life in prison, with up to 50 years of incarceration for his convictions.

As for my cousin's friend, she suffered nerve damage but no memory loss. The bullet remained lodged in the top of her skull.

Chapter 7

Some of my other cousins were taken from their parents at a young age. Their only choice was to either enter into the system or be taken in by family members. I knew anything was better than being a part of the system, and living in foster homes. At the time, I wasn't mature, intelligent, nor responsible to guide them peacefully and respectfully. I was dealing with my own personal situations. But I felt bad because losing one parent is unbearable for anyone. And the thought of knowing the other one was locked up in prison for life, would make things worse.

My uncle worked as an Armed Security Officer for Lagarda for 10 years. He must have enjoyed his position to carry it for a decade. He was stationed at the local welfare offices. Back then it was rare to have a carrying a concealed weapon (CCW) or Concealed Pistol License (CPL) but he had both. His presence brought peace to the family. And plus he was the oldest of all his brothers, so he gained major respect. Work for him was an outlet to meet and greet the community and to protect the interest of the staff. He always kept his work and personal life separate. My uncle enjoyed his family and took care of the financial needs. Usually, the mailman dropped off mail at routine times, so everyone knew when to check their mailbox just in case a paper check was in the mail. One particular day my uncle grabbed the mail from the mailbox; it was a couple of bills. He opened the phone bill to see the balance. While flipping through the pages he noticed a lot of outgoing calls to strange numbers that made him curious. He knew he hadn't placed the calls, especially at the times they were made. My cousins were getting ready to go outside to play but were disturbed by shouting. Instead of walking out the door they walked toward the commotion, it was their parents arguing. They were going back and forth about who paid what bills in the house.

My uncle felt because he paid the bills she didn't have the right to disrespect him by calling other men from the house phone. It forced my uncle to monitor her activities more to see if she was mistreating him. Every month the phone bill came, he rushed to open them and the call log had fewer outgoing calls. After a while, he felt things were getting back on track with them, so he stopped looking at the phone bills altogether. Later on that year, he noticed she was smiling more. She had a bubbly attitude toward situations that would usually upset her. She also went out of her way dressed to impress. So one day, my uncle came home early from work, and my aunt had programmed my cousins to tell him that she was out with some of her girlfriends. She left without preparing a meal for them, so they were hungry. With no food to eat, they walked around the corner to a friend's house. Hours later my uncle made it home earlier than expected and found the

Joy M. Pierre

kid's home alone. He didn't understand what the urgency was, because of how long the kids said she had been gone. But all they could tell him was what she said, she would be back soon. My cousins hadn't eaten, and cell phones weren't popular at that time so he couldn't get ahold of her. He paced the floors, going window to window to see if she was walking down the street. He even walked out on the front porch to see if he saw her coming. She was nowhere in sight. It puzzled him. My aunt knew what time he usually made it home from work, so she came back home before he would have. But that day when she came home, he was in the living room waiting.

She was surprised to see him and an argument broke out while the kids were watching. Furniture chairs were pushed over throughout the argument. My cousins were watching and crying, they were scared. The arguing continued until my aunt said that she wouldn't leave the kids alone anymore and would stop chatting with other guys. My uncle found no trace of her affairs with other men, but as soon as he let his guard down she was back making phone calls and using online dating sources. My uncle saw her behavior change back to her old ways. She had my cousin's lie for her so he wouldn't get mad. As usual, he confronted her because he loved her and wanted her to change.

One night my cousin rushed to prepare himself for school. He needed a little playtime to make a pop-up tent. He creatively thought to assemble it by using a sheet and a portable fan. It was going to be his bed for the night. With a smile on his face, he crawled in proudly and laid down, trying to fall asleep. It was hard because he heard yelling and screaming. Out of curiosity, he jumped up and left out of the room. He saw my uncle and was stunned.

My aunt was on the floor screaming and crying the word no. The volume of her cries were louder when she saw my cousin enter the room. She didn't want him to see her like that. My uncle was standing in the hallway toward the entrance of the living room. He was loading a shotgun with multiple bullets. He aimed the barrel at her looking through the scope. My aunt reached her hands toward my cousin calling him to come to her. Naturally, he ran to her and sat on her lap. My uncle lowered the gun because my cousin was positioned in the center of the target mark. My aunt never took her eyes off my cousin. She continued crying telling him how sorry she was, but my uncle cut her off from talking. He never moved from the spot he was standing, telling my cousin to come to him so that he could get out the way. It confused my cousin because while he was walking away, my aunt reached to snatch him back, but my uncle kept telling him to come. Still screaming and crying my aunt was telling my cousin not to leave her while she called his name repeatedly. He didn't feel he was going anywhere, and was doing what he was told. It was like the game monkey in the middle and he was going back and forth. My uncle used a stronger tone telling my cousin to come addressing him by the name son. He knew he meant business when he said that. So my cousin slowly walked toward him, and my uncle demanded that he got his sisters and left the house. He ran past him to get the girls. They were in their room. None of them had on pajamas, just long t-shirts that belonged to my uncle. At the same time my aunt was on her hands and knees crawling into their bedroom, begging for her life. He didn't let her out his sight, so he walked behind her. As soon as she made in the room the gun cocked and he shot her.

My cousins looked at each other and zoomed to the front door. Before they made it out of the house, the gun

Joy M. Pierre

went off again, he shot her a second time. They snatched the door open and ran out the house, through the yard, clothesless and barefoot. They heard louder screams and then another shot. After the third shot, everything went silent.

They kept running until they ended at a friend's house. They balled a fist pounding the windows, but it was after midnight so everyone was sleep. Their only option was to hide in the bushes of a vacant house next door. In shock, my cousin and his two sisters remained hidden in the bushes. He didn't know if it was safe to come out. Plus, my uncle ordered him to take the girls and leave. He stayed close by, so he could be found when my uncle called for him. Peeking out the bushes, he saw my uncle being escorted to a police cruiser with his head bowed and his hands cuffed behind his back. That was a moment he never imagined. My aunt laid helpless on the gurney, with blood everywhere. The response team pumped her chest while transporting her to the ambulance. My cousin and his two sisters left the bushes going back to the neighbor's house. They balled fist pounding louder on the doors and windows again. That was their only option, they had nowhere else to go. Someone opened the door in awe asking them what they were doing outside at that time of the night, without clothes on. The neighbor ran for the phone to call the police to report a disturbance from the kids. Officers came to interrogate them, but my cousin was scared and didn't answer any questions.

He didn't know what to say or believe. That was a traumatic moment for him. Child Protective Service (CPS) came to get them. After realizing they had no clothes on, the CPS worker took them to a Meijer's, a one-stop shop on Pierson Road to get clothes, socks, and shoes. She also wanted them to relax and open up with her, so she took them to McDonald's. As much as they love McDonald's she picked the wrong time and day to take them.

She asked multiple questions, and my cousin was mute. His mind was empty trying to digest everything he just witnessed. A phone rang, and he looked up at her. It was her facial expression. Even though my cousin wasn't talking he saw the worry on her face. She hung up the phone with glossy eyes telling them how sorry she was. They weren't understanding, so she said it again. Then she told them that their mother died on the operating table. They couldn't stop the bleeding and they also tried putting her back together but wasn't successful. From that moment forward, my cousin shut down. The cashier heard everything that was said and gave him free food anyways to show her concerns. The CPS worker took them to her office and asked more questions. She knew my uncle would be convicted, but had hopes of their mother's survival, so they could go home. But there had been a change of plans when they announced her death. They were asked if splitting up was an option, which it wasn't. They were all each other had. The CPS worker respected their wish. She went out of her way to purchase more clothes, and socks since they weren't allowed to go back to the house. Not knowing what the next step was, my cousins, hung out with the CPS worker all day until it was time for her to go home to her personal life. She had a family of her own to tend too.

Secretly, they stayed in her office with coloring activities and movies. It was a bathroom in there so food, games, movies, pillows, and blankets were provided to them free by the CPS worker that cared for them all within a day. That night they made themselves comfortable sleeping on couches and floors. It was like being away from home at a slumber party. But the worker felt by them being there it was better so they weren't split up. The next day came, they were still there. The day after that, still there in her office. She grew attached, from caring for them at work wishing a way to keep them herself. So in that short period of time, she tried to adopt them. She knew it wouldn't be long before someone found them hiding away in her office or came looking for them. She knew the severity of the consequences if she was caught. She kept them anyway, putting her job in jeopardy. The following week some of our family members went to get them. The CPS worker was saved, but heartbroken.

Come to find out, days before my aunt's death she wanted my cousin and his sisters to lie for her. She also wanted them to help her find other men from dating sites, so they all could be against my uncle. She knew if they helped her she had a better chance of getting away with online dating. She showed them pictures of other men from the site and told them the men were their next daddy. Out of anger my cousin jumped up and unplug the phone cord from the wall. The internet connection was lost. She blurted out calling my cousin a bastard. He didn't back down and told her he knew who his dad was. Her eyebrows raised. She looked down to grab the closest object in reach. There was pens, papers and books on the computer desk. She grabbed an animal dictionary and flung it at his head to hit him, but he turned around and took off. It hit him in the center of his back. She was angry. My aunt told him she was going to put him into foster care, and that my uncle would never see him again. From the threat, he knew he couldn't tell my uncle because he would have been in trouble. He knew what it meant to be in foster care and didn't want to live with another family.

The next morning he got up early. He ran out the front door to my uncle's car and hid in the back seat, without anyone noticing. My uncle jumped into the car and took off heading to work. Through many stop signs and stop lights, my cousin stayed low, not to be seen. My uncle pulled up to his job, he grabbed his things from the front seat and got out. He walked toward the building but saw something from his peripheral vision. My cousin was caught. My uncle was shocked to see him, asking what's wrong because he was crying. He was panicking, telling him that my aunt was trying to give him away. It was unbelievable for my uncle to hear. He took him back to the car and gave him a hard strawberry candy to calm him. But it only did so much because my uncle drove him back to the corner of their street. My cousin was told to run home and not tell my aunt where he was. So when he got home he lied and said he was with friends around the corner. He still was in trouble, but not to the extent he would have been, if she knew he told.

That evening after work my uncle fell on the floor by the front entrance. He was holding his chest gasping for air. Not caring, she mumbled and walked past him out the front door. My cousin ran to his aid asking what was wrong, but all my uncle said was he needed help. My cousin ran to grab some water and a pillow, but that didn't help. He told my uncle he was coming back and ran out of the house around the corner to a friend's house to get their dad. Making it back to the house, my uncle laid helpless on the floor. They knew something was wrong but not exactly what, so my cousin called 911. He made it to the hospital and was told he had a stroke and a heart attack at the same time. The staff told my cousin if it wasn't for his quick response, my uncle wouldn't have made it.

My family knew all these stories well because they constantly spoke of them at gatherings. In my younger days I knew to leave the room when grown folks were talking. It was the way of keeping a child out of grown folks business. But I still listened to the conversations as I passed through, anyway. There were times I stood being nosey at the corner of doors, listening until they realized I was there. I never repeated any of the stories, they were just exciting or interesting.

As for my cousin, we kept in touch with each other. Once he told me, it was only a few people in his life that could calm him down, and I was one of them. As proud as I felt to be his cousin, I felt bad too. I had a part in knowing who was going to take over his life. I asked my family to keep him and his sisters together, thinking it was the best decisions. And when it happened I became jealous of him having the person in his life that I wanted in mine.

From recognition and information, I learned that after his traumatic experience, life didn't get any easier, and I blamed myself for many years. I use to tell myself, only if I kept my big mouth shut, some of the bad times could have been prevented. But after maturing, I still made an impact in his life. We both were abused mentally, physically, and verbally. We also lost a parent at an early age. And we also experienced some things we had no control of. But from all of that, it shaped me. I didn't feel alone anymore because I knew someone else that experienced tragedies too, and it made me feel more human.

Chapter 8

I thought of another mysterious story when police officers stopped at donut shops, grabbing donuts and coffee just to make time go by. Since Flint was so small, we knew most of them personally. But in the summers, anything you could imagine went down. Out of all the crimes that happened in the city, shooting folks was number one on the charts. Flint never challenged other cities in crime rates but always managed to be one of the five worst cities in America. Mostly everyone carried guns for protection. And retaliation remained the mentality. Some kids accidentally shot themselves and other people from showing off or pretending to be gang bangers. Many people in the city lacked knowledge and understanding because they didn't do right by their education.

When General Motors took over Flint, high school diplomas or degrees weren't required. So many in the city dropped out of school and worked for the auto industry to make a decent living for their families. As the shops closed, crimes filled the city as a replacement because there weren't enough jobs to keep the city from falling into poverty. Many became unemployed or leaned toward the streets to survive. So when the police officers weren't at the donut shops, there were in the streets investigating homicides.

In the summer of 2010, a couple of cops were cruising the streets. It was late at night when they saw a strange pile of clothes from a distance. With one of their hands on their holsters and the other one holding a flashlight they slowly walked toward them squinting their eyes. Not knowing what they would find, it was a man in a pool of blood. There was no one around who witnessed the gruesome attack. He was barely breathing and was continuously losing blood. Before he passed out, he mumbled telling the cops it was a white guy. They looked in his pocket and pulled out a wallet that identified who he was. But the strange part was that there was cash in there too, and he hadn't been robbed. They rushed him to a nearby hospital with multiple stab wounds. And on the way, he lost consciousness and died. I thought it was another statistic for being in the wrong place at the wrong time. And it was the norm to hear that people died on the way to hospitals because of all the killings. During the investigation, there were no other leads that helped them figure out what happened.

The location where he was found was busy, but late nights were deserted. The victim was liked by many and didn't seem to have enemies. From his appearance, he was short and slim. He looked like the ideal person who wouldn't put up a fight with anyone. Being outdoors alone in the city of Flint was enough to make you a victim. With little evidence to go on, there was a store nearby that had a surveillance camera that showed the same

Joy M. Pierre

SUV riding by in both directions. But wasn't enough to identify the make, model and year of the vehicle. Investigators went through records realizing there was a pattern to the stabbings that took place a week prior. It was many black men that were assaulted in the middle of the night walking alone.

They recognized that the stabbings started months before. But they considered the first attack gang-related so the story died out with no exposure. A month later, a second victim had a similar pattern. He was a black man walking at night alone, who was stabbed too. Gun violence was the highest percentage of crime in Flint, so the stabbings were drawing major attention.

I felt a maniac was on the loose, stabbing folks like he was Michael Myers because they were happening more. The city was at a standstill. Being stabbed and slashed open was a new tactic that none of us expected. Different crews called around asking, who was the mastermind behind those horrific, senseless stabbings? I can also remember some of my friends and family stayed home because it was safer than being out at night. So we ran all our errands during the daytime. Even my regular late nights at the club were on hold too. That was scary. Men feared for their lives, keeping up with the local news to see which neighborhood was next. Just about everyone in the city had some gangster in them and appeared to be tough. That was the reason why walking alone was never a fear for any of us. The crime scenes were so gruesome that he lifted victims from the ground with the blade ripping it upward toward their chest. He had to be strong because it would have taken a lot of strength to tear through the body like he did. By then, six was stabbed with three dead, and investigators still had no suspects. There was another body found in a parking lot with stab wounds making the attacks more familiar. That victim wasn't robbed and had two wallets that weren't touched. Investigators realized there was a connection between the attacks. There was an attack that happened every night for a week straight. It didn't seem like he would stop because more victims were coming up dead. The more attacks there were, the more the city became concerned.

The city panicked from all the crime scenes shown on the news. People were afraid of becoming the next victim so everyone imposed a self-curfew to stay safe. Everyone including The Flint Police Department wanted to get to the bottom of all the crimes, but no one was communicating because they were happening in different jurisdictions. The different task force came together forming a group to catch the suspect. But even with them all they still weren't getting anywhere. All they could tell the city was, the suspect was a white male, strong, drove an SUV, carried a knife and seemed to attack black men at night. That could have been anyone.

One victim in the hospital spoke to detectives, telling them how he was stabbed by a guy walking down the street. He didn't realize he was walking up to the attacker. The attacker stopped him and asked for directions to a specific street. While he was pointing him in the direction, the attacker was acting like he couldn't hear him so he got closer like he was about to hug him. The victim pushed him away, and he felt the pressure from a sharp object yanked out of him. He grabbed his stomached and noticed the blood and realize that he got stabbed. He ran off holding his stomach, knowing he would be chased. But the attacker just stood there waiting and watching. He was losing tons of blood and felt weak, so he ran to the first house he saw with a porch light on. He used his bloody hands to bang on the door, which helped save his life because he knew it was only a matter of seconds before he would pass out.

I'm sure if he didn't have that blood stamp on the window, the strangers wouldn't have opened the door and let him in. They kept him responsive until EMS arrived, taking him to the hospital. I thanked God he survived the attack because he could give a complete description of the attacker. He described him as a big wrestler, with a baseball cap on that had beady eyes. He stood 6'5 and weighed 280 lbs. They spread his photo all over the news giving the city some leads on who to be on the lookout for. By then he attacked fourteen black men and was under the impression of being racist. The city was already in fear, but when they found out race could have been a factor, the fear turned into rage. Most of us in the community forgot that the city was predominantly black and we walked the streets at nights, more than any other race.

The more victims that survived, the more investigators knew they had the same suspect. All the victim's stories were just alike. On some occasions the suspect drove at night hiding his actual size. He camouflaged himself in the darkness, asking victims to come closer to the car. When they walked near he asked for directions, or if they knew how to fix a car. And while they were explaining, he caught them off guard sticking them with his dagger. He took advantage of the men that looked kind-hearted or the men he could overpower. Days past and with no suspect, the investigators reached out for help. They opened a 24-hour hotline for tips. The city came together and gave helpful leads for them to follow-up on. A few days past with no attack. No one knew if he was on their street, in front of their homes, or in lines with him at grocery stores. It was a waiting game. We waited for him to strike again.

I can remember hearing stories from some women teasing their men because they were home at a respectful times. I believed there was no late night rendezvous. It didn't worry them about their mate catching them; they were more worried about getting caught and stabbed by the attacker and ending up dead. Everyone changed their routines. That was the only time I saw everyone in Flint united, or at least they pretended to be. Occasionally I glanced at my surveillance cameras when I heard cars riding up and down my street. Even though I was a woman, I made sure I was home by nightfall so I wouldn't be caught outside my house. I didn't take him for granted. He could have diverted and targeted women and children too.

The investigators thought they spooked him and was on the run because the city was quiet. He hadn't stabbed anyone and all the other city crime was at a halt. As awkward as it sounds, it was like they wanted another stabbing to occur so they could gain more information. He was a professional like he done it before. He stayed off the radar, maybe plotting, hiding or running. The police sent out bulletins because they still needed help. A police department in Virginia contacted the slasher task force in Flint with a similar attack. They told them that a victim was walking at night, and a man standing by his vehicle stopped him, asking if he could help fix his car. The victim leaned under the hood but saw movement from his peripheral vision. The attacker swung a hammer, trying to kill him. But he somewhat moved, and the hammer pounded the hood of his SUV leaving a dent. The victim ran away.

There were three attacks in four days. It was unusual because the small city had no crime. He hurt the victims but none of them died. They gained a major lead from

Joy M. Pierre

the last hammer attack. A shopping center had newly installed cameras and caught him in the act. But to be certain they had the right vehicle they went to multiple hotels looking to see if they saw a vehicle with an out-of-state license plate. With no luck, Virginia put out their own bulletin to locate the vehicle. They also wanted information about other similar attacks to make sure it was the same suspect Flint was inquiring. Not only was Flint and Virginia in a panic, it was other states too. Overnight the story went national, alerting the nation of the attacker and his routines.

I couldn't believe he was in Virginia hammering folks with the same methods he used in Flint. The city of Flint heard he had jumped states, saying if he came back how they would take him out. Everyone had photos of him and the vehicle he owned. I wasn't intimidated by all the things I've been through in my past, but he, on the other hand, was spooky. The men in the city feared him, so I knew he was a big deal, and if he was to come back and been spotted, they would have dealt with him.

When I thought the attacker was lying low in Virginia, another attack happened. A black man was standing outside of a building. He was approached by a stout middle-aged man that asked for directions. As the man stepped closer, pointing him in the direction, a knife was shoved into his stomach, stabbing him multiple times. It caught the victim off guard because he was defenseless and didn't see it coming. Still, with no witnesses, the attacker walked away leaving him to die in Ohio. I couldn't believe he started in Flint, done attacks in Virginia, and stopped in Ohio attacking more. I wondered if he was on his way back to Flint because it sure looked like it. His tactics drew lots of attention because of the blazer, and the vicious stabbings against black men.

When the Flint task force received a call from Ohio describing the same tactics and behaviors, they knew the crimes were connected. Now that the attacks were taken place in different states, the FBI got involved because they didn't know how to stop him. One victim he stabbed 2-weeks ago in Flint, had recovered from fighting for his life, in the ICU. He gave his description of the attacker that was critical. The attacker had a logo on his t-shirt that described an alcohol beverage, and he wasn't a white man as described. It was shocking because the entire time everyone was on the lookout for a white man. Flint learned that the attacker was a different race, so we didn't know who we were looking for at the time.

Someone called a tip into the task force as an unidentified caller. The attacker supposedly worked for a store seconds away from Flint's city limits. She knew he went to Virginia to visit family the week of the stabbings. Police followed-up on the tip and saw the store was selling those t-shirts that one victim described. They approached the counter to speak with the owner, and showed a sketch of the attacker to him. Not only did he verified the person, he also provided them with his first name and a current photo. He was working under the table for cash, so the owner didn't have the last name to provide to the authorities.

So with eighteen stabbings from multiple states. The task force was closer to their target. They had his name, a photo of him and the vehicle. The investigators were closer to the target than the city of Flint realized because they got his phone number from a co-worker. They didn't realize that they had a copy of his license on file from a sting operation. They ticketed him for selling liquor to minor's weeks prior.

That man was busy. He was getting tickets, stabbing folks, and being a good employee. Who would have ever known?

Hours later after receiving tips, the attacker was at the airport in Atlanta, Georgia waiting at a boarding gate to fly out of the country. Investigators had him paged over the intercom to get him alone and away from other passengers. They didn't want to draw any attention toward him. They wanted an easy capture, and hostages were the last thing they wanted him to have. The attacker didn't realize that the authorities were there to arrest him. So he sat there waiting to board the plane.

Later we found out the attacker flew from Michigan to Kentucky where he was pinged close to an International airport. They didn't know if he was traveling by air or driving down major highways because he was close to both. The authorities checked the list of passengers traveling for that evening and found his name. He was on his way trying to leave the country. Authorities knew they only had moments to stop him. If he would have boarded the plane, it would have been too hard to get him extradited back to the United States.

The task force worked with the prosecutors and the judge for a warrant. They contacted authorities in Atlanta, GA for help. Because of the severity, they placed an undercover swat team feet away from his departure gate. They wanted a perfect capture. While under pressure that late night made it difficult for everyone to connect. To make a valid warrant everyone had to be available. The most important part of the warrant was the judge's signature. He had to sign it, give it back to the prosecutor so they could release it to Atlanta. They finally released the warrant, and continued to monitor him on the airport cameras. As he sat waiting to board the plane, authorities suspiciously moved in on him. They knew they only had minutes to seize him allowing no room to escape.

Back at Flint, the task force had high anxiety. They knew the attacker was big and dangerous. Atlanta notified the task force. He was at the departure gate and authorities had him surrounded. Hundreds of miles away with no visual looks, it felt like torture to them. It was one thing to be front and center, and another thing to play the waiting game, not able to act. They looked at each another quietly expecting the capture. You could hear a pin drop. That's when they heard Atlanta say they had him in custody. Everyone cheered with relief, feeling the nightmare had ended.

Piles of bricks were lifted off me too. He came out of nowhere and went on a killing rampage in the city. Later after his capture, I found a more in-depth article about his past and his stabbing escapades. The task force had his complete name and a photo of his actual face during the investigation. The attacker was a 33-year-old Arab, born and raised in Israel that came to the states in his teens after his father died. He lived in Virginia. After he had a physical confrontation with a family member, it forced him to move to Flint. Back in Israel authorities learned he stabbed someone there too.

When his sketch was released. The city thought it was a good description of him but it wasn't. His actual photo looked nothing like the sketch and that was the reason no one could identify him. I felt they only gave information to soothe us over.

The surviving victims said a muscular white man asked for directions or asked for help when he approached them. The police said when the victims got close he stabbed them without saying a word like he was a psycho. And from my understanding, they described him as a 6'5" white guy that weighed 280 lbs. But police said he was a 5'11" to 6'2" white guy that weighted between 180 and 210lbs. That was a major difference, and I see why he wasn't caught.

I remember hearing they didn't have information on his whereabouts and they didn't know he left the state until the stabbings occurred. But the police identified him as the liquor store worker. And they tracked him through several states from his credit card usage. All of that was hard to believe.

Later I found out he was arrested twice during the stabbings. But officers didn't know they had a serial killer in custody. The police had arrested him during a traffic stop in Virginia after officers saw he had an outstanding warrant for assaults. He had a knife and a hammer in his truck then, but since they weren't prohibited to have, they let him go. That was very shocking.

Whether all of information or facts were correct. We never found out because the attacker never gave us closure on his reasoning. I lived in Flint during that arduous time and was affected by the tragedies. I knew what it felt like to live in fear and be surrounded by anxiety with no outlets. In Flint, the only way to survive was to watch your back, and be prepared to defend yourself. What a wicked web we weave when we practice to deceive.

Chapter 9

We all have or had experienced a relationship whether it was a friend, mate, co-worker, or allies. And I had encountered many of them growing up. Just to feel loved, when my friends were assigned house chores by their parents, I jumped in and helped too. It was the only way I coped with my jealous heart of not having any responsibility and recognition from my dad. He remarried after my uncle was locked up for the murder of his wife. It wasn't a problem he remarried, but he never mentioned his intention of getting married, so we felt disowned. It hurt because I thought his kids meant the world to him. The feeling of not being present on his big day was dreadful, but what we experienced after that was bold and ugly.

My sister and I were living in the house my mother bought when my grandfather passed away. Momma knew she had nothing growing up, so she tried to establish a place for us to call home. My dad, on the other hand, saw things differently. My sister and me both worked second shift, so we were gone all day and came home at nights. One night I made it home just before she did. I put the key in the door and pushed it open. I reached for the light switch and turned it on. No lights came on, I flickered it up and down still nothing. I didn't remember where the spare light bulbs were and I had no flashlight. I didn't know what to do, so I called my sister to tell her that I was on the porch waiting for her. She came home, and we walked in together. She went in one direction and I went into another. There was no beeping, from any of the appliances. No clocks were flashing to alarm me there was a power outage. There was no electricity flowing through the house. The both of us were confused because she paid the bill. We grabbed a few things and headed back out and crashed at different friend's houses, waiting to call the power company in the morning. When morning came, my sister called me with disappointment in her voice.

She was fussing and I couldn't understand; she was talking too fast. The anger in her voice alarmed me that something was terribly wrong. So I met her at home because it wasn't like her. We sat at the dining room table and she told me that someone had called the power company to cancel the service. That was confusing. We reached out to our dad. His voice carried, so I could hear everything. The tone of his voice made me believe he was shocked. I thought we had no enemies, but I could clearly see someone was playing tricks on us. I was staring at her. She hung up the phone. Wrinkles formed in the middle of her forehead. She had the look of worry all over her face. I said nothing because I didn't have an answer to fix the problem. It disappointed her when my dad told her he didn't do it, so she called him back. That time she asked to speak to his wife. It puzzled me why she wanted to speak to her. I heard him speaking loud, yelling her name. I didn't hear him mention who was on the phone, but he could have warned her by whispering that it was my sister. His wife said hello. My sister didn't hesitate. She asked why was the power turned off. Then there was silence. I kept moving my ear closer to the phone but still couldn't hear. My sister yelled telling her she was wrong and had no business doing it. I moved closer and held the phone with her, wanting to hear. They both were yelling back and forth which made me confused. We already didn't have a relationship with her, and I felt by them arguing would make things worse. My sister hung up the phone and slammed it down on the table.

That's when I learned about how easy it was for others to control you. Things went downhill from there. Weeks later, we came home from work. Our normal routine was to chat about our day. My sister followed me into the kitchen and I grabbed a pot from under the cabinet, and a pack of Raman Noodles from the pantry. I turned on the kitchen faucet. Our talking stopped. I twisted the knob again in the opposite direction. We opened the cabinet where momma had lodged a bullet hole to see if the water valves were off. The knobs were still on, so water should have flown out perfectly. We looked at each other having a suspect in mind. Instantly, my sister called my dad's wife knowing she was argumentative, putting blame on her. I didn't care for all the squabbling, but the longer my sister kept her on the phone, the more his wife came clean. It was haunting to know that someone hated us for no reason, and it was also painful that my dad didn't get involved.

When my sister hung up the phone, she told me we were spoiled wenches, and that's why our water was cut off. I shouted telling her she was wrong. It confused me, wondering why she would say that about us. But my sister reassured me that those weren't her words, but it was a message from my dad's wife. It was unbelievable, but I believed her because she never took out the time to get to know us.

Months passed, my sister checked the mail as usual and found a postcard that said we had certified mail that needed to be picked up from the post office. They addressed it to me and my sister with a strange word "et al." attached. I couldn't understand what it meant, or what they meant by it. We knew someone was up to no good because of what we previously experienced.

I wished the mail carrier would have never delivered that postcard to our house. But we were brave, so we went to the post office wondering what it could be because we owed no one money. My sister handed over the postcard to the clerk, and she brought back a white envelope that required a signature. She signed it and we walked away. She tore the side open, snatching the letter out. It was a court summons addressed with my dad and his wife's name vs. my sister, me and the rest of the family to appear in court. Our eyes bucked and our mouth dropped. We read more walking over to the wall, leaning against it. We looked at each other speechless. I looked at the top of the summons again. It devastated me because I felt he turned his back on us.

There were only weeks before the court date. It limited my time, because I was already struggling to balance life and work, and then I had to prepare myself for an unknown day at court. So adding it all into the equation was overwhelming. I had never stepped foot inside of a courtroom. So, more time would have allowed me to prepare mentally and physically.

The day came, we made it to the courthouse. We walked to a courtroom that had a list of trials outside the door with our names on it. That was the courtroom we entered, seeing our dad and his wife sitting faced forward. They hadn't noticed we walked in. We sat on the opposite side. The long hard uncomfortable bench made me tense. It felt like I was being watched.

I sat listening to other court cases while we waited. I kept looking up at my sister hoping she knew what was going on. I felt I wasn't the smartest, but I was somewhat clever, so, I knew if my sister understood the terminology we would have been okay. It would have eased our mind, to answer questions better because I hated to be humiliated.

Every time a court case was over, my heart pounded, thinking we were next. So when they finally called our names we stood looking over at my dad, watching him stand too. He didn't look well, but he had to be well enough to appear in court. I stood staring looking him head to toe. They walked toward the back of the courtroom so my sister and I followed. But it was strange because it was the opposite direction of the judge. There were two sets of double doors and we walked through one. Off to the left was a small room with a table. That's where we sat. I sat in front of him squinting my eyes. There was something wrong with him, and I felt it. The counselor began to talk and my mind drifted off in the days, not paying attention to him. I wanted an explanation as to why we were taken to a private room like it was a secret. I snapped back listening to the conversation. They were discussing how our water and power was shut off because we weren't paying rent. Before my dad moved out, he told us to maintain the bills only, so that's what we did. Momma had bought the house for the family and I felt that was the reasoning behind it. Then it was mentioned that we were behind in rent for an entire year and needed to pay $4,800. I really didn't think she wanted the money but she did know between my sister and I, that amount of money couldn't be paid.

Back then I was only making six-bucks an hour. That would have taken me an eternity to help pay. My dad jumped in and said no just pay for the court fees. His wife looked at him amazed. They couldn't have been on the same page because she thought he would sit there and say nothing. I blurted, we shouldn't have been there in the first place, which stunned everyone because I was always a thinker, not a speaker. Others knew it as a quiet spirit but my facial expression told its own story about my mood. The original court order was for possession of the premises. The court denied the request because we hadn't signed a lease agreement, only a water affidavit. As proud as we were to be present and stand up for ourselves, we had a home to go to. But we knew it was only a matter of time until she thought of more ways to torment us.

Out of respect for my dad, indifference overruled love, and to keep down the commotion between us all, we voluntarily moved out months later. That how my sister ended up in Pontiac, MI alone, leaning on a man for help. Me, on the other hand, I stayed in Flint working three part-time jobs to survive. And moved to a place I couldn't afford that forced me into a shelter.

All the time we lived together, I felt we should have grown a closer bond. But we lived two separate lives wanting the complete opposite. Because my mom was deceased, I tried to get more attached to him. I knew whatever he liked would interest me too. Unintentionally he taught me what I wanted in a man. And that was how to accept love. I never saw him abuse anyone, but I experienced it. I also learned how to process feelings and handle disagreements. Back then I could only have a relationship one way or the other. It was either I found someone with his unhealthy traits, or someone the complete opposite.

But I thought if I dated someone opposite of him, I could have a healthier relationship. So that's what I did. I found someone that was understanding and calm. There were many days we laughed with each other for no reason at all. It felt good to have someone around and not be alone. I thrived for someone who had their own identity. But the longer we got to know one another, it revealed he wasn't the one you would call obsolete. Those peaches and creams I had with him turned into a bloodbath.

It was a Friday that I was at home with one of my friends. We chilled at the times when I wasn't with him. We sat on the porch with my sisters and their friends. Bill Collins pulled up and it looked like he was having a bad day. Normally I was happy to see him, but not that time. I received a phone call from a person I knew nothing about. He left to visit his hometown in New Jersey for a week. Somehow his baby mama found my number in his phone and called me with unexpected drama.

She told me that she knew everything about him and me and that he was moving back to Jersey to live with her because she was pregnant. I saw no competition for that. He was about to have his second child with her, and I had none. I took that phone call as a warning, thinking our relationship was over. I didn't answer none of his phone calls, so that's why he popped up because he felt I was rejecting him.

Indeed I was mad but when seeing his presents, I felt his baby mama was wrong about him because he came back. I didn't lower my guard, playing hard to get. I knew if I didn't see him he would be out of sight, out of mind. But by him popping up it made my night harder. He walked over to me and I stood up. I felt he would make a scene so I walked toward him. He asked why I haven't called him. And I just looked at him because I was still mad. My facial expressions told him the answer. I was standing my ground because I wanted him to take me serious. He asked another question, so I pretended to ignore him. He repeated himself asking where I was going for the night. That's when I responded with an answer that I knew he wouldn't approve of.

It was already late, so I walked back toward the porch where I heard my sister and her friend's sniggling. I looked at them frowning making my way inside the house to fix my hair. He walked in behind me. An argument broke out because I told him I was going to "Da Spot" on the west side of Flint. It was a hood club on Dupont Street where anything and everything went on.

I felt he was having his cake and was eating it too, and I knew his family back home wasn't out of the picture. So I didn't let him change my mind. I walked outside onto the porch and he came out behind me mumbling. I stood on the porch and he kept walking until he made it to his car. He jumped in, slamming the door. I looked at him squinting my eyes. He cranked the car and revved the engine, grabbing all our attention on the porch. Everyone looked at me asking what was wrong with him but all I said was he didn't want me hanging out.

He backed out the driveway squealing his tires hopping the curb. He put the car in drive and sped off, burning rubber. I was embarrassed because none of us saw him like that. I wanted to tell my friend I changed my mind, but the peer pressure wouldn't let me back down. I felt like he spoiled the chance for me to go out. I didn't think the matter was serious for him to get mad. Then I thought, why did he get so mad? Maybe he wanted things to change and didn't know how to change them. From the emotions of my friend ready to go, I got in the car with her, slamming the door. I knew what he did was wrong, but I felt I was wrong too, and it made me no better than him because I was playing games too. We drove up the street to the corner store. I saw Bill Collins' car, so he had another chance to persuade me on why I shouldn't have been going to the club.

We jumped out of the car, slammed the doors walking toward the entrance of the store. I reached for the door handle and jumped back because it was swinging open. It was Bill Collins pushing the door open. He didn't acknowledge me continuing to walk past. He was mumbling. The neighborhood guys saw my friend and me, and they raised their tones. I stood in one spot listening because the mumbling turned into an argument. I was looking in both directions trying to figure out what happened, but Bill Collins kept walking toward his car. The neighborhood guys were standing in the line facing the door. Then I heard vulgar language.

My friend and I didn't have a clue what was going on. So, I went after Bill Collins calling his name, but he ignored me, continuing to walk toward his car. Before I could get to him, he opened his door, got in, and slammed it. I slowed my pace because I knew he was still upset. He put the car in drive and slowly pulled out of the parking spot. I yelled telling him to wait, but the car kept rolling. He had to have heard me because he stopped just before he pulled out of the store's driveway. I ran up to the car asking him what happened. He spoke with profane language telling me that the guys in the store were idiots. And how every time he went to that store they picked on him for no reason. The guys in my neighborhood were overprotective over the block and weren't friendly toward outsiders. So, if you didn't grow up in our hood you weren't welcome. And I kept him away from them the best way I could. Bill Collins continued by saying how they didn't know him like that. I cut him off so he couldn't speak anymore by telling him they were jealous because he had nice cars and was from a different state. Then he yelled that it wasn't his fault that they lived in the hood. The more he talked, the more his voice raised. I heard someone say come on, so I turned and saw the guys walking out the store. He saw them too. He looked into his rearview mirror focusing his attention on them. I grabbed his face turning it toward me. I told him not to be mad at me, and he could come over when I got home. He was still saying he didn't want me to go but said okay, anyway.

I smiled at him leaning my head inside the car to kiss him, not realizing I was about to kiss him goodbye. I heard a gunshot, which shattered Bill Collins' driver's side rear door window. The bullet flew past my right ear popping my eardrum. All I could hear was a ringing tone. I bent down on the side of the car while the shooting continued. I was screaming and crying the whole time, realizing what was happening. My life was flashing before my eyes. Bill reached down in front of him to grab his gun from under the driver seat, but he couldn't reach it. He was getting shot repeatedly. When I saw his body move from the force of the bullets, I knew I was shot too. There were many people at the store so there was a lot of commotion going on. My friend was in the front of the store yelling my name. I looked back and took off to the front of

Joy M. Pierre

the store. My friend asked if I was shot and I told her no looking down at myself.

Everyone fled the scene, leaving the parking lot deserted. Many doors slammed and the smell of burnt rubber filled the air. I ran back to the car looking at Bill Collins slumped over in the seat. I yelled, call the police, but no one responded. I looked behind, but it was only my friend standing there. Bullet holes were everywhere. I looked at the ground and saw shattered glass from his windows. Reality had sat in. I yelled his name asking him if he could hear me, but he didn't respond. So I screamed louder, holding on to the door frame. I didn't touch him because I knew he was already in a lot of pain and I was still in shock. So I stuck my head inside the car continuing to scream but he didn't flinch. I knew he was dead, so I rubbed his head gently from the front to back.

My sister was supposed to be at home but somehow she was behind me tugging on my arm. She was pulling and dragging me away from the car, but it was like we were playing tug of war with each other. She told me I shouldn't see him like that while she pulled me one last time. She was rescuing me from the nightmare, forcing me to go home. I couldn't leave him there alone. It was no one there to help him, but the more she tugged on my arm and talked to me, convinced me.

Someone notified us that the ambulance took him to the hospital. So we all jumped in the car and drove there. I sat in the waiting room, annoyed; I had a headache, which felt like someone struck me with a sledgehammer with full force.

My family and friends made the situation worse because they kept talking about it. I was tired of them repeating what I just experienced. I sat patiently, hoping to see him. I wanted to talk to him, just to hear his voice to make sure he was okay. But no one came out to update us of his condition so we sat in the waiting room, waiting. The longer I waited, the more negative thoughts I formed. I knew none of it was my fault, but I wished I didn't act despitefully. I remembered all the guys' faces, but I didn't see which one did the shooting.

My dad found out that someone shot Bill Collins, and he was in the hospital. He was out of town, so he came back to see what happened. For some reason, he seemed to like him or maybe it was because he occupied my time, so I wasn't bothering him. As supportive as my dad wasn't, I was glad to see him, but he let me have it. He lectured me about going to the neighborhood store because it was dangerous. I pretended to listen even though my mind was focused on what just happened. I thought nothing he said made sense. That store may have been dangerous and there have been plenty of shootings, but I didn't realize it would touch home like it did. I grew up in that neighborhood and lived there since I was five years old. I knew the neighborhood well. That was back when you knew everyone on your block by their first name. I thought the community stuck together, but I was sadly mistaken from the love I wasn't shown.

Nothing was a secret in the city of Flint. Bill Collins' mother flew in from out of state. She wanted to talk to me for a while. She was a pretty, caramel-skinned lady, with her hair wrapped in a scarf like a Muslim. Her accent made it complicated for me to understand her when she spoke. I told her about our relationship. But the entire time she rudely told me I wasn't good enough for her perfect son. She felt it was my fault he'd gotten shot and was mad that he wanted to live in Flint because of me. She

Joy M. Pierre

claimed I had done enough, which was heartbreaking. She continued, telling me that he had a girlfriend back home who had one child by him and one on the way. That was confirmation he had another life in New Jersey. She was planning to take her son back home and said I wouldn't be able to see him because she changed his name. My dad went to see him while she spoke to me alone. But when he came back her tone changed, and she was nice.

She told my dad she didn't want me to see him like that. It confused me listening to her. When I was alone, she said she didn't want me to see him anymore, but told my dad a different story. I knew from there on they'd never accepted me into their family. I left the hospital and went home.

I felt myself slipping back into my old routines. I spent the rest of the weekend, moping and feeling empty. The following week, I pulled myself together because I wanted answers about the shootings. So I went to the police station. While I was there, I remembered they had some of my belongings that I left in the car. So I spoke with a detective that handled the case and he told me after we chatted he would release my personal items. I followed him back to his desk, and on one side of the room, a man was sitting in handcuffs, screaming he didn't do it. And on the other side was a couple arguing back and forth with a clerk. I knew I wanted answers, but the environment was uncomfortable. I sat in a seat at his desk looking over my shoulders. I didn't want to be there, but I was hoping they would shed light on what happened from their investigation.

The detective opened a folder. He held up a photo asking if I saw it before and I did. It was a picture of the car he was driving, the night of the shooting. He continued to question me in more details. He asked if I knew where he purchased the car, but all I said was no. I knew he drove the car from New Jersey, but that was it. He insisted that I told him the truth because my fingerprints and belongings were all over the car. I panicked because I didn't understand what the big deal was about his car. I stared at him saying nothing, squinting my eyes. Then he closed the folder and told me after the shooting, the police ran his license plate and discovered that the car was stolen from an airport. He didn't say which one. He couldn't have been talking about the same person I knew. I never mistook him for a thief.

If that was true, I felt misled and deceived. Then I thought that could have been why he was secretive on the phone with his family. My mind was all over the place. I felt he could have only taken the car two ways. He could have rented a car and never returned it. Or he could have swiped keys from a hotel valet parking without permission. But then I thought, why didn't I think about that before? Was I that naïve? I had to have been. I knew he had two brand new cars of that same year, with no executive jobs. Then I thought, how did he afford those luxurious cars? Since I knew nothing about his secret life, I wasn't in trouble, but it troubled me he added me to his crew without my recollection. Thank God, the police never pulled me over, because I could have been handcuffed, embarrassed and put in jail over something I didn't know.

I wondered if I had gotten pulled over, would he have let me take the blame or was he into me enough, to tell the truth? Most of the people I knew in similar situations took the fall for someone else's mistakes. There was more. I found out he was also wanted for check fraud too. I put my elbows on his desk, shaking my head. It devastated me. I wasn't any help to them, but they were helpful to me. I found out his true identity.

The detective stood from his chair, telling me if I knew any more information, to come back. So, I stood too. He walked me down a long hall at the other end of the building. He took his keys out and unlocked the door. It was the evidence room. With widened eyes, there were guns everywhere. I knew the number one crime in Flint was shootings, but the number of guns they collected was unbelievable. He walked me to the back of the room, and I saw a handgun that looked familiar. I kept thinking it was Bill Collins gun, but it wasn't. It looked like the gun momma had. Tears rolled down my face as the officer asked if I was okay. I told him I was having a bad day. I saw my cell phone and wiped my tears remembering why I was there, in the first place. I grabbed it making sure it was intact by inspecting it, but nothing was missing. I thought to take a few other things that didn't belong to me but was distracted by a paper that caught my eye. My name and address was on it, so I snatched it, and was glad he didn't tell me about his secret life.

About a month later, my friend who was with me that night was at the hospital seeing her brother in the ICU. She called me and told me she knew where Bill Collins was. I jumped up from a chair pacing the floor getting more information. The next day we both went to visit her brother. We made it to the floor, and I was overwhelmed. I knew I was wrong because I was sneaking inside to see him without permission and I wasn't letting anyone stop me.

As we went through the ICU double doors, my heart pounded. I looked at my friend and she gave me a grin. She showed me where his room was, and I walked past it slowly, peeking. Continuing to walk, I didn't have enough courage to go in there alone. But, I knew the staff would have been suspicious if we walked into his room together.

I went to her brother's room for a while to think of a plan. I told my friend I was leaving and would be back. I walked out of the room and no one was paying attention. I walked down the hall, hoping to see Bill Collins, but I knew I couldn't walk inside the room and get caught. I didn't want to see him in his present condition, but I knew, if I didn't face what happened, I couldn't move on. Nurses were all around me, so I took a deep breath, walking nonchalantly until they turned their backs. I kept thinking I couldn't get caught. So I made it close to his door and ducked into his room, so I wasn't seen. He was awake and alone. They wrapped his body like a zombie. No one had groomed him so he looked like a caveman. I recognized him but he didn't look like the same person I knew. I only had seconds to be there. I walked toward the head of the bed, smiling; I thought I'd never see him again.

He smiled back moving his lips, but I couldn't hear anything. I nodded my head saying no because I couldn't hear him. He kept moving his lips until he got frustrated because he was trying to talk and couldn't. I told him not to get frustrated, and I snuck in because his mother didn't want me to see him. I also asked him for his real name. His lips mumbled. Then, he moved his lips again, but I still couldn't understand.

I got frustrated because our time was limited. His lips mumbled again, but I couldn't understand. It was hard to read his lips. I kept asking him to repeat his name until I understood. I smiled repeating his name back. And he nodded yes. I told him I had to go before someone saw me and I ran out of the room. I made it back to my friend brother's room exhaling. I couldn't believe I saw him. I knew since his mother thought everything was my fault; I had no hope of seeing him again.

Weeks later, my phone rung. I answered. It was his aunt calling asking me to come down to the hospital. Bill Collins wanted to see me. I headed for the hospital, I couldn't help but wonder if I was being set-up so his family could belittle me? At the hospital, his aunt greeted me in the lobby, since she thought I didn't know his name. I kept my secret and went along with her plan. We rode up to his floor in the elevator. The ride up made me dizzy, from the pressure. Still not trusting her, I kept looking behind me to see if someone followed me. We walked down the long hallway to the ICU, through the double doors. I had visions of myself passing out or breaking down into a crying spell.

At his door, I took a deep breath before entering the room. I saw him sitting up in the bed watching me walk through the door. His aunt grabbed her belongings and left us alone to talk. He had recovered well. The last time I'd seen him, he couldn't talk to tell his side of the story. But the truth came out when his voice came back. I was free at last. He told everyone how that night went and I had nothing to do with it. He was happy to see me but sad to say he would not see me anymore. And that he wanted to see me one last time to say his goodbye before moving back home. I was in tears. I told him we could work things out.

He told me he had a family at home he was going back to. He also said he didn't want me to spend the rest of my life taking care of him because of his condition. I told him that none of that mattered. Then he told me that the guys had paralyzed him. I was speechless. He told me that the doctor said there was a possibility he could walk again but he had a lot of work to do. I stared at him with glossy eyes. I knew it wasn't my fault. But, for some odd reason, I thought, if only I hadn't planned on going out with my friend, that night could have been prevented. I left the hospital because I felt he was at peace with his decision. I couldn't believe they paralyzed him. Jealousy almost took his life. I wondered how those guys would have felt if they knew he wasn't a drug dealer when they thought he was.

I knew we met for a reason. I learned a valuable lesson behind it all. I took him for granted, thinking he could replace my voids. He, on the other hand, took advantage of me because I was vulnerable. So we lived a toxic life from the lack of communication and secrets. The relationship problems we faced had no intent on being fixed. He found me, when I was broken and without peace. I limited myself and focused only on the negativity. I had no visions or big dreams. I had no faith and didn't believe in hope. But I learned the hard way. Through the pain, I lost trust and confidence in others. Some learn fast, and some learn later in life and some never learn. So I learned to stop letting the wrong one find me in peace, and leave me in pieces.

Joy M. Pierre

Closing

Well, just to tone things down. In this book, I had no intentions of hurting anyone's feelings. And the names were omitted to protect their innocence. The book was an invitation to show others we all have a past, but the past doesn't have to define who we are today. There are many of us who are hurting but are afraid or ashamed of exposure. You're not alone. Many of us are like you and me.

My life has had many bumps and bruises. I know every family has a story, but this was my story and I had to reorganize things based on the facts of my life as I saw them. This life shaped my personality. Through it all, I lost family to traumatic experiences. And now I also lost touch with lots of great people because of my busy life as a wife, mother, sister, and most of all child of God. I didn't give up on communicating with others because everyone needs someone to confide in at times. It's understandable to focus on achieving your goals, but remember not to lose yourself in the process, it's valuable.

I learned we look at others and judge them based on appearances, upbringings, race, and nationalities. That's selfish and hateful. And hatred doesn't grant us any additions to life, it actually destroys us from the inside out. So while we may think we're better than others or have more than the next, what makes us better than them? We all made mistakes and have dirty laundry in our closets. We all strive for excellence, but none of us will ever become perfect. Life is a journey and we should depend on one another for fulfillment. Don't underestimate others. They may know more than they say, think more than they speak, and notice more than you realize. Respect yourself so others will respect you as well. Show love by, caring, and being a genuine mate, friend, and leader. Be open to learn new ways.

Don't judge a choice without understanding the reasons. I live a square life for the safety of my family. But I realize that life happens at the end of our comfort zone, and none of us are exempt from being at the wrong place at the wrong time. So guard your footprints and never take life for granted. Because each and every experience we all face can be our last.

In my Exquisite Past, my mom and dad didn't have the greatest relationship, but in life, we only react to situations based on our upbringings. As I matured, I learned not to fault them for the lack of knowledge in their parenting. Blaming others turns into bitterness, which could turn into sickness to our health, and can endanger our body when we hold grudges against others. As for my sister, brother, and I, we still find it difficult to cope with one another because of the emotions that were attached to holidays. The wounds that pierced my heart were never

Joy M. Pierre

forgotten, but from my past experiences I chose to guide my children in opposite directions, because they are our future. Unfortunately, I grew up around guns, and I paid a high price from choices that were embedded into my lifestyle. My life could have been taken many times, but my purpose in life overpowered death. So, I live an honest, humble, respectful, caring, sharing, joyful, and most of all thankful life. None of my tragic experiences will be forgotten but I'm leaving them all in the past.

"Love is free and it doesn't cost a cent."

I'm hopeful that my memoir touched your heart and changed your perspective on how we judge one another. We never know what the next person has been through, and all the struggles they have faced to get to where they are today. I smoked, I was an alcoholic, I tried committing suicide, I experienced sexual abuse, and I was homeless at one point in my life. No matter what you are going through, remember someone could be in a worst predicament than you. Life is a precious gift, and shouldn't be taken for granted. So what I couldn't express myself and was misled by my family. So what I was a loner and didn't have the best parental guidance. I allowed fear and denial to control my life for a long time. Now, I speak loud because I have a voice to remind others that they do have a chance in life to overcome stress, depression, loneliness, low self-esteem, and remind them we're great from inside out, not outside in. All we have to do is stand on faith, and believe. So if you feel your back is against the wall because you didn't achieve a level you felt you deserve, it's all a life journey so that you can help others who have been through some of the same experiences. I understand your present circumstances may feel as if God has given up on you, but remember he loves you and is waiting with open arms to take your burdens away and give you peace.

So I'll ask you one last time,

"What cost are you willing to pay to live an additional year? And do you think guns kill people or do you believe it is people that kill people?"

1 Corinthians 13:4-11 Amplified Bible (AMP)

4 Love endures with patience and serenity, love is kind and thoughtful, and is not jealous or envious; love does not brag and is not proud or arrogant. **5** It is not rude; it is not self-seeking, it is not provoked [nor overly sensitive and easily angered]; it does not take into account a wrong endured. **6** It does not rejoice at injustice, but rejoices with the truth [when right and truth prevail]. **7** Love bears all things [regardless of what comes], believes all things [looking for the best in each one], hopes all things [remaining steadfast during difficult times], endures all things [without weakening].

8 Love never fails [it never fades nor ends]. But as for prophecies, they will pass away; as for tongues, they will cease; as for the gift of special knowledge, it will pass away. **9** For we know in part, and we prophesy in part [for our knowledge is fragmentary and incomplete]. **10** But when that which is complete and perfect comes, that which is incomplete and partial will pass away. **11** When I was a child, I talked like a child, I thought like a child, I reasoned like a child; when I became a man, I did away with childish things.

Motivation

I give total praise to God almighty, who is my refuge, my fortress, and the leader of my life. Without him none of my memoir would have been possible. He delivered me through my broken days. And my memoir is also my testimony. I received healing and forgiveness from His love, guidance, and strength. I'm also thanking him for comforting me during the good and bad times. And also for giving me a discerning heart. The Lord is my Shepard, and I shall not want or be afraid. He will direct my paths for the rest of my life.

Giving thanks and love to my husband, who is my rock. And for every day and night that I tried giving up on my dream, because of my busy schedule. His patience comforted me, while I relived my Exquisite Past. He was also supportive in all my decisions. I also thank him for our teamwork, friendship, and our relationship as a spouse. Thanks for all your support and I love you with all my heart.

Entering the Life of the Exquisite Past

Giving thanks and love to my children, they're a great motivation. I also want to thank them for all their encouraging words. My heart goes out to them because they remind me that parenting is a major key to their success.

Giving thanks and love to my sister, who is the most amazing woman I know. We been through it all and it has been a long road for us. We lived through many experiences together. The hardest part of our journey was, we never forgotten any of our tragedies. The arduous road we took made us the women we are today: strong, bold, courageous, and faith bound.

Giving thanks to my brother, who is the best. He is a strong man that keeps a strong mind through life's journey. I love how we communicate by keeping one another lifted in our dreams. Our lives, which were also contentious, helped us find the right direction and made us look forward to becoming successful.

Rest in Peace

Marjorie, Markeda and Artavia Byas, and the rest of
the family and friends who rest in peace.

None of you will ever be forgotten

Entering the Life of the Exquisite Past

www.ingramcontent.com/pod-product-compliance
Lightning Source LLC
Chambersburg PA
CBHW020356130626
46549CB00006B/2308